Withdrawn

startup weekend

How to Take a Company
from **Concept** to **Creation**
in 54 Hours

MARC NAGER
CLINT NELSEN
FRANCK NOUYRIGAT

WILEY

John Wiley & Sons, Inc.

Published by John Wiley & Sons, Inc., Hoboken, New Jersey.
Published simultaneously in Canada.

For general information on our other products and services or for technical support, please contact our Customer Care Department within the United States at (800) 762-2974, outside the United States at (317) 572-3993 or fax (317) 572-4002.

Wiley publishes in a variety of print and electronic formats and by print-on-demand. Some material included with standard print versions of this book may not be included in e-books or in print-on-demand. If this book refers to media such as a CD or DVD that is not included in the version you purchased, you may download this material at http://booksupport.wiley.com. For more information about Wiley products, visit www.wiley.com.

Library of Congress Cataloging-in-Publication Data:

Nager, Marc, 1985–
   Startup Weekend: how to take a company from concept to creation in 54 hours / Marc Nager, Clint Nelsen & Franck Nouyrigat.
      p. cm.
ISBN: 978-1-118-10509-2 (cloth)
ISBN: 978-1-118-15963-7 (ebk)
ISBN: 978-1-118-16023-7 (ebk)
ISBN: 978-1-118-16024-4 (ebk)
   1. New business enterprises. I. Nelsen, Clint. II. Nouyrigat, Franck. III. Title.
HD62.5. N335
658.1'1-dc23   2011024064

Printed in the United States of America.

10 9 8 7 6 5 4 3 2 1

This book is dedicated to entrepreneurs.
Because of you, the world is a better place.

Contents

Foreword

Carl Schramm and Steve Blank

The Art and Science of Startups in Revolutionary Times

In the future, we will look back at this decade (2010 to 2020) as the beginning of an economic revolution as significant and world-changing as the Scientific Revolution of the sixteenth century and the Industrial Revolution of the eighteenth century. We are currently standing at the beginning of the *entrepreneurial* revolution. This doesn't mean just more technology-based products (though we'll certainly get our share of those). Rather, this is a revolution that will permanently reshape business as we know it, and more importantly, change the quality of life across the entire planet for all who come after us. And organizations like Startup Weekend are at the very forefront of this groundbreaking development.

The Barriers to Entrepreneurship

Over the past 40 years, startups continued to innovate as each new wave of technology took hold. However, the *rate of innovation* was constrained by limitations we are just beginning to understand. Only in the past few years have we come to appreciate the fact that startups in the past were constrained by factors like:

1. Long technology development cycles (how long it takes to get from idea to product).
2. The high cost of getting to first customers (the cost to build the product).

3. The structure of the venture capital industry (that there were a limited number of venture capital firms, each of which needed to invest millions per startup).
4. The expertise about how to build startups (which was clustered in specific regions like Silicon Valley, Boston, and New York).
5. The failure rate of new ventures (startups had no formal rules, and were frequently *hit or miss* propositions).
6. The slow adoption rate of new technologies by governments and large companies.

Fortunately for us, many of these elements have changed drastically in recent years. Not only are technology cycles speeding up and the cost of getting products to customers decreasing, but organizations like Startup Weekend are pushing knowledge and networks to greater numbers of entrepreneurs.

The Democratization of Entrepreneurship

What's happening is something more profound than a change in technology; the change is in the fact that the many inhibitors and limitations to startups and innovation are being removed. All at once, starting now.

Compressing the Product Development Cycle: In the past, the time to build a first product release was measured in months or even years, as startups took time to execute the founder's vision of what customers wanted. This meant that they built virtually every possible feature the founding team envisioned into a monolithic release of the product. Yet time after time, startups would find that customers didn't use or want most of the features *after* the product shipped. The founders were simply wrong in their assumptions about customer needs, and they wasted considerable effort developing all those unused features.

Fortunately, today's startups have begun to create products differently. Instead of building the maximum number of features they can imagine, they look to deliver a *minimum feature set* in the shortest period. This lets them launch a first version of the product to customers in a fraction on the time. In fact, for products that are simply *bits* delivered over the web, a first product can be shipped in *weeks* rather than *years*.

Startups Built for Thousands Rather than Millions of Dollars: Startups traditionally required millions of dollars of funding just to get their first product to customers. For instance, a company that developed software would have to buy computers and license software from other companies and hire the staff to run and maintain it. A hardware startup had to spend money building prototypes and equipping a factory to manufacture the product.

Today, open source software has slashed the cost of software development from millions of dollars to thousands. No consumer hardware startup has to build their own factory, as the costs are absorbed by offshore manufacturers. And the cost of getting the first product out the door for an Internet commerce startup has dropped by a factor of *10 or more* in the last decade.

The New Structure of the Venture Capital Industry: The plummeting cost of getting a first product to market, particularly for Internet startups, has shaken up the venture capital industry. Venture capital used to be a tight club clustered around formal firms located in areas like Silicon Valley, Boston, and New York. While those firms are still there and growing, the pool of money that invests *risk capital* in startups has expanded, and a new class of investors has emerged. New groups of VCs called *super angels*, which are generally smaller than the traditional multihundred-million-dollar VC fund, can make the small investments necessary to help launch a consumer Internet startup. These angels make lots of early bets and double-down when early results appear. And the results *do* appear years earlier than they would in a traditional startup.

In addition to super angels, *incubators* like Y Combinator, TechStars, and the 100-plus others like them worldwide have begun to formalize seed-investing. They pay expenses in a formal three-month program, while a startup builds something impressive enough to raise money on a larger scale.

However, the penultimate events in this area are Startup Weekends: 54-hour conferences that allow developers, designers, marketers, product managers, and startup enthusiasts to come together to share ideas, form teams, build products, and launch startups.

Startup Weekends have also emphasized the fact that venture capital and angel investing is no longer a U.S. or Euro-centric phenomenon. Risk capital has emerged in China, India, and other countries where risk taking, innovation, and liquidity are encouraged on a scale previously only seen in the United States.

The emergence of these incubators and super angels have *dramatically* expanded the sources of seed capital. And this globalization of entrepreneurship means the worldwide pool of potential startups has increased *at least tenfold* since the turn of this century.

Entrepreneurship as Its Own Management Science: Over the past 10 years, entrepreneurs began to understand a critical fact: Startups are *not* simply smaller versions of large companies. While companies *execute* business models, startups *search* for a business model. Or perhaps more accurately, startups are a temporary organization designed to *search* for a scalable and repeatable business model.

Therefore, instead of adopting the management techniques of large companies, which too often stifle innovation in a young startup, entrepreneurs began to develop their own management tools. Using the business model/customer development/agile development solution stack, these individuals first map their assumptions (in other words, their business model) and then test these hypotheses with customers in the field (customer development) and use an iterative and incremental development methodology (agile development) to build the product. When founders discover the assumptions that are wrong, as they inevitably will, the result isn't a crisis; it's a learning event called a pivot—and an opportunity to change the business model.

As a result, startups now have tools that speed up the search for customers, reduce time to market, and slash the cost of development.

Consumer Internet Driving Innovation: In the 1950s and 1960s, U.S. Defense and Intelligence organizations drove the pace of innovation in Silicon Valley by providing research and development dollars to universities, and purchased weapons systems that used the valley's first microwave and semiconductor components. In the 1970s, 1980s, and 1990s, momentum shifted to the enterprise as large businesses supported innovation in PCs, communications hardware, and enterprise software. Nowadays, however, government and the enterprise are followers rather than leaders. Today, it's the consumer—specifically, consumer Internet companies—that drive innovation. When the product and channel are bits, adoption by 10s and 100s of millions of users can happen in years versus decades.

The Entrepreneurial Singularity: The barriers to entrepreneurship are not just being removed. In almost every case, they're also being replaced by innovations that are speeding up each step, some by a factor of 10. For example, the time required to get the first product to market at Internet commerce startups has been cut by a factor of 10, as have the dollars needed to get the first product to market. Additionally, the number of sources of initial capital for entrepreneurs has increased by a factor of 10, and so forth. And while innovation is moving at Internet speed, this won't be limited to just Internet commerce startups. It will spread to the enterprise, and ultimately, to *every other business segment.*

When It's Darkest, We See the Stars

What does it mean that we are at the cusp of a revolution as important as the scientific and industrial ones? Revolutions are not obvious when they are happening. When James Watt launched the Industrial Revolution with the invention of the steam engine in 1775, no one said, "This is the day everything changes." When Karl Benz drove around Mannheim in 1885, no one said, "There will be 500 million of these driving around in a century." And certainly in 1958, when Noyce and Kilby invented the integrated circuit, the notion of a quintillion (10 to the 18th power) transistors being produced each year seemed ludicrous.

Yet, it's possible that we'll look back at this decade as the beginning of our own revolution. We may remember this as the time when scientific discoveries and technological breakthroughs were integrated into the fabric of society faster than they had ever been before, or when the speed of how companies operated changed forever. We may recall it as the time when we reinvented the U.S. economy and our gross domestic product began to take off, and the United

States and the world reached a level of wealth never seen before. It may be the dawn of a new era for a new U.S. economy built on entrepreneurship and innovation. Startup Weekend is at the forefront of this revolution: a grassroots movement that brings technology, tools, and networks to the people who are most committed to creating positive change in the world. In short, this era may be the one upon which our children will look back and marvel that when it was the darkest, we saw the stars.

Preface

WHAT MAKES A successful startup? Blood, sweat, and tears (and fun) may help, but they alone can't do it all. Entrepreneurs need to put together the right team, with members who have complementary skills. They need to receive constant feedback from customers. They need to trust their partners and empower the people who work with them. They need to learn on the job, and consistently work to understand the marketplace.

Over the past three years, we at Startup Weekend have seen these things happen over and over again. We have been amazed at how much people can accomplish in the course of 54 hours at Startup Weekends across the world. Some people walk out of their first weekend session with a cofounder, seed money for the next several months, and hundreds of customers already signed up for their product or service. For most of our attendees, though, Startup Weekend is only the beginning. It is just the start of an exciting and demanding learning process that they will continue to experience in the years to come.

In the pages that follow, our goal is to take readers through the actual experience of Startup Weekend—what it's like to pitch your business idea to 200 strangers in 60 seconds; how teams struggle when they discover that other people have had similar ideas; what it's like to see how well someone works and how much they know within hours of meeting him or her; and what it's like to meet some of the most experienced and successful mentors in the startup world.

As much as we want anyone with a desire to explore entrepreneurship to attend Startup Weekend, we recognize that not everyone will. Therefore, this book will try to take the lessons of Startup Weekend and distill them for a larger audience. In the subsequent chapters, you will learn valuable information about pitching your ideas for businesses with others, finding the right team to make your enterprise a success, the value of experiential learning, taking your customers' and the market's pulse (even before your product is ready for launch), using different startup models for project management, and making the best use of your startup time—whether you are ready to become an entrepreneur for the weekend, or for the rest of your life.

Acknowledgments

Writing a book is a big endeavor and we would not have been able to accomplish it without the support of the Startup Weekend community. From the written and oral stories alumni and participants shared with us to the feedback we've received at every stage along our journey, this book is the result of hundreds—if not thousands—of individual contributions. Although there are too many people to thank individually, in a very real sense, every Startup Weekend participant has made their mark on our organization; therefore, although anonymous, they are essential pieces of the story.

The entrepreneurs who shared their stories with us are listed by name below. We cannot express how grateful we are to those alumni, friends, and supporters who shared their Startup Weekend experiences. We have tried to include everyone and we apologize if we've forgotten to name anyone.

We would like to extend a heartfelt thank you to the supportive and resourceful team at John Wiley & Sons, Inc. Particular recognition goes to our editor, Dan Ambrosio, and our development editor, Christine Moore. We would also like to recognize Naomi Riley for her assistance with the manuscript.

To the Ewing Marion Kauffman Foundation, we cannot express how grateful we are for what you've done to support and promote Startup Weekend and thousands of other passionate entrepreneurs throughout the United States.

We would particularly like to thank Carl Schramm and Steve Blank for all they have done and continue to do to support entrepreneurs. We are honored to work with you.

We would like to thank our Board of Advisors: David Cohen, Bo Fishback, Eric Koester, Dan Martell, Danielle Morrill, John Sechrest, and Nick Seguin; and the Startup Lawyer, Ryan Roberts. Your guidance, constructive criticism, and unstinting support have helped grow this organization in ways we never thought possible.

Startup Weekend would be nothing without our rockstar team of global organizers. Every day, you guys remind us why we're here and what a small group of dedicated and engaged people can accomplish. Each one of you is an integral part of our community—long live the Startup Weekend Mafia!

Similarly, we would like to thank our amazing network of Community Advisors: Adam Philipp, Bob Crimmins, Bruce D'Ambrosio, Buzz Bruggerman, Charlie O'Donnell, Ed Kimm, Greg Gottesman, John Cook, Jonathan Berger, Kal Vepuri, Marcelo Calbucci, Mark Merich, Matt Shobe, Meng Wong, Mike Koss, Nate Wetheimer, Neil Patel, Rebecca Lovell, Roy Leban, Shaherose Charania, Sherry Reynolds, and Tony Bacigalupo.

To all the mentors who have shared their advice and best practices with us over the years, thank you so much. The following list is by no means complete: Andy Sack, Bill Warner, Brad Feld, Dave McClure, Denis Browne, Eric Ries, Jessica Livingston, John Lewis, Jonathan Ortmans, Kathleen Kennedy, Mark Suster, Robert Scoble, and Yosi Vardi.

We'd be remiss if we didn't acknowledge the huge impact our global sponsors have had not only on the organization but on the thousands of Startup Weekend alumni, too. Thank you to Amazon Web Services (Rodica Buzescu), oDesk, O'Reilly, Microsoft BizSpark (particularly Juliano Tubino, Julien Codiniou, Ludo Ulrich, and the rest of the global team), Sun Microsystems (particularly Jeremiah

Shackelford), TokBox, and Twilio. Another round of thanks is also in order for the regional and local sponsors who help us bring our events to cities around the world.

A huge thank you goes out to the Startup Weekend Core Team: Keith Armstrong, Jennifer Cabala, Anca Foster, Ashley Hodgson, Maris McEdward, Joey Pomerenke, Tawnee Rebhuhn, Shane Reiser, and Adam Stelle for their belief in and commitment to our vision. You guys are awesome! We would especially like to thank Maris McEdward for her dedication and hard work throughout the book writing process. We mean it when we say that we couldn't have done it without you.

Finally, we'd like to thank our family, friends, and girl-friends. It's been a long and sometimes unexpectedly bumpy road but that's never stopped you from supporting us and believing in what we were creating. And, of course, we'd like to thank Andrew Hyde, who made all this possible to begin with.

Contributors

Adam DeLong

Alex Farcet

Alexa Andrzejewski

Alexis Ringwald

Amir Harel

Anders Hedberg

André Reuba

Andy Dragt

Angie Chang

Antonios Manessis

Anuranjita Tewary

Arantza Uriante

Arthur Nisnevich

Bastien Serafin

Bedy Yang

Bert-Jan Woertman

Beth Altringer

Brian Labarre

Brian Zeuercher

Cameron Kashani

Charlie O'Donnell

Chris Eben

Christian Blavier

Clara Martin

Clement Cazalot

Colleen Brady

Dan Rockwell

Dan Schamir

Daniel Knoodle

Danielle Siauw

Dash Dhakshin-
amoorthy

Dave Angulo

David Smallbone

Don Caruso

Don Ritzen

Donald DeSantis

Eli Hayes

Elizabeth Grigg

Elyssa Ludher

Eric Jorgensen

Eric Lagier

Evan Buxbaum

Evgeny Pogorelov

Francesco
Mancusi

Frank Denbow

Friederike Welter

Gabe Pelegrin

Hélène Durand
Couppel de
Saint Front

Humberto Lee

Ian Hunter

Imo Udom

James Briant

James Digby

James Hobbis

Jason Armishaw

Jason Reynolds

Jean-François
Vermont

Jeff Martens

Jeffrey Paine

Jeremy
Haberman

Jeremy
Lightsmith

Jeremy Monat

Jerry Suhrstedt

Jesse Maddox

Jim Benson

Jim England

John Britton

Jon Rossi

Jonathan Berger

Jonny Lee

Kenny Nguyen

Kevin Leneway

Kevin Owocki

Kris Fuehr

Kyle Ellicott

Kyle Kesterson

Lesa Mitchell

Leslie Mack

Liang Shi

Liesbeth Vriens

Lorraine Ball

Ludmilla
Figueiredo

Maria Encinar

Marshall Hayes

Matt Talbot

Matthew
Titsworth

Matylda
Czarnecka

Maya Bisineer

Megan Molino

MeLinda McCall

Melody Biringer

Michael Coates

Michael Irizarry

Michael Leow

Michael Maddox

Michael Marasco

Michael Pastko

Mike van
Hoenselaar

Mike Vandenbos

Mikey Tom

Nathan Bashaw

Naz Rin

Nicholas Gavronsky

Nick Burke

Nick Martin

Nick Seguin

Nico Habraken

Norris Krueger

Oksana Yaremchuk

Olivier Desmoulin

Pankaj Jain

Particia Araque

Philippe Gelis

Randy Hook

Rebecca Lovell

Richard Grote

Roland Gröpmair

Roy Leban

Sasha Pasulka

Scott Weiss

Sean Kean

Seth Samuels

Shane Mac

Sherwood Neiss

Stefano Orowitsch

Steven Thrasher

Therese Hansen

Thibaut Labarre

Thubten Comerford

Tim Gasper

Toke Kruse

Tyler Koblasa

Vivian Tian Na

Wendy Overton

Willy Braun

Yaniv Feldman

Introduction

Why Starting Up Is All about Trust and Empowerment

Marc Nager, Clint Nelsen, and Franck Nouyrigat

Marc Nager and Clint Nelsen

Imagine you had a great idea for a new business. Maybe it's the next Facebook, the next Twitter, or perhaps something more mundane—the next grocery delivery service or no-mess toothpaste tube. You think about it when you wake up in the morning and when you go to bed at night. You jot down notes about it periodically throughout the day while at your regular job. Maybe you tell your husband or your roommate a little nugget of the idea here, or you read something in a magazine that gets you excited about it all over again. When the weekends come, you daydream a little, maybe even tinker with a business model or search online to make sure that no one else has come up with this scenario already. To be honest, you're a little nervous that by the time you come up with the hours and the money to make a go of your idea, someone else will already have made it a reality.

Now, imagine you walk into a room of perfect strangers and have to pitch your idea to the crowd in 60 seconds. The people who like it might decide to work on it with you and the ones who don't, well, they'll just go off in their own direction. Would you do it?

Most people would think twice before taking this plunge. After all, you've been working on this idea for such a long time—and it is *such a good idea*. What would happen if the people who walked away decided to steal the idea and use it to start their own company? Or what if the people who wanted to work with you really wanted to take the idea in a new direction and it didn't end up looking the way you had imagined?

At Startup Weekend, we have two words of advice for you: *Let Go*.

Every weekend at events around the country (and around the world), budding entrepreneurs come together to share their ideas—their *babies*—with people they have never met before in the hopes of making these fuzzy plans a reality. Trusting others completely—for their feedback, their advice, and their help—is the only way to accomplish this.

It used to be the case (before we took over) that people attending Startup Weekends had to sign nondisclosure agreements (NDA), promising not to reveal the ideas they learned about to anyone outside. This model did not really sit well with us or with many of our participants. A few people actually left an event early because of the NDA requirement, and went to a nearby coffee shop instead—where they had their own little Startup Weekend. That's why, to this day, we prefer to operate in a kind of open-source mind-set.

Of course, it takes people some time to get used to this attitude. People are often hesitant in the first couple of hours of a Startup Weekend, and will only share a little bit of their idea. They approach others tentatively, inquiring about their skills but also holding back information, while offering only a proxy of their idea. Most people are also a little nervous about whether their idea is good enough—since they have barely exposed it to the light of day, let alone the critical minds of a hundred strangers.

Are you ready to share your startup ideas?

- If so, what type of feedback are you most looking for?
- If not, what is holding you back?

But then, something changes. They see one person doing it—explaining the whole idea, openly, honestly, trustingly—and they ask themselves: Really, what's the worst that can happen? You'll get some negative feedback? That's a *good* thing. If there is a fundamental flaw in your business model, or if someone has done this before, then you'll find out and you can move on with your life, and to the next idea.

Pretty soon, people start to trust each other with their ideas, and the whole room begins to exude energy. It's like watching popcorn pop. People start heating up with the passionate thoughts and plans they've been keeping inside. The bowl, as it were, becomes filled, with fresh, hot ideas. It's one of our favorite moments.

As codirectors of Startup Weekend, we like to say: "There are no brilliant ideas, only brilliant execution." Or, as one of our Startup Weekend attendees, Jerry Suhrstedt—CEO of Northwest marketing agency Heavy Guerrilla—put it recently, "Ideas are a dime a dozen."

If none of that makes sense, then think about it mathematically, and consider the following example. Someone who was working on an idea alone came to us a while back. He was trying to start a business for months while keeping it a secret; at one point, he was running out of cash. "I'm in big trouble," he confessed to us. "I don't have enough money to turn this idea into something." We told him it was time to take his idea out of hiding. After all, if you don't talk about your idea to anyone, the probability of finding a customer or an investor is zero.

One participant at a Startup Weekend in Olympia, Washington, really understood this notion. After attending one of our meetings, he wrote to us that by the end of Friday night, a group of 40 people had come up with 10 excellent ideas for marketable products and services. He explained, "From Red Panda [an energy drink marketed to yoga studios] to Drunk Test [an iPhone app that would test your level of cognitive function with a series of questions], all of the ideas could be worth pursuing, if someone had the motivation or interest." Of course, as he quickly realized, "Coming up with ideas is easy. The next [and more difficult] step is *doing* something about it."

In fact, a lot of our participants have found that it's actually easy to get stuck in the brainstorming phase. This doesn't surprise us; coming up with ideas is fun, as is telling other people about your ideas and getting their feedback. As the same participant observed, "This process of generalizing an idea, adapting it slightly, and then refocusing on the new idea is something that the human brain is optimized for." It's easy to just keep doing that over and over again; but it's not a very good way of creating a functional startup. The key to the startup is to, well, *start*. Just pick an idea—any idea. They're all good. And then get to work.

We have found that that famous Nike slogan—*Just Do It*—might apply to launching companies even more than it does to accomplishing athletic feats. Another participant, Willy, told us that the first time he attended a Startup Weekend, he had an idea but decided not to pitch it to anyone. He explained, "I'm rather quiet and shy, so I first chose not to pitch. [I felt there were] too many folks looking and listening and judging. It was just too much. In fact, I hardly had the courage to attend the weekend." But after listening to a few of the pitches, Willy decided it was worth the risk. His idea didn't sound worse than any of the other ones: "So I gathered all my strength and went on stage, which I did regret for some *very* long seconds. But there I was. I won't tell you it was easy, because it wasn't. I stammered; I lost the perfect sentences that I'd prepared;

and I'm 100 percent sure lots of people thought: 'God, this is crap. What does he want to do?' But, hell, I had wonderful feedback about my ideas."

How Trust Led Us to the Greatest Adventure of Our Lives

It's not easy to trust that other people will listen openly to your ideas and then help you improve on them. But it's the way Startup Weekend began.

In the spring of 2009, we—just a couple of unemployed Seattle-based marketers—went on a road trip. One of Marc's former colleagues had gotten a job in Qatar and needed to sell his car in Seattle, Washington, so Marc offered to drive the car from Seattle to the new owner in Denver, Colorado. He called up Clint (who didn't really have much to do at the time), and within a couple of hours, we were on the road.

One year earlier, we had participated in a Startup Weekend in Seattle. At the time, Startup Weekend was a for-profit company that charged people about forty dollars to attend events. The events had corporate sponsors; everyone in attendance worked on one project together and the participants were offered a form of stock options when the weekend was over. However, this model wasn't working very well. The company was losing money, and the SEC wasn't very happy about the stock options part either.

So, we got to talking about ways the model could be improved. A couple of hours outside Denver, on what turned out to be a life-changing road trip, Clint told Marc that he had a phone number for Andrew Hyde, the then-CEO of Startup Weekend in Boulder, Colorado. We called him on a lark and stopped by, and Andrew was all ears. He was more than supportive. And then he did something pretty amazing; he said, "Why don't you guys just go ahead and take Startup Weekend over?" We were more than a little taken aback by the level of openness and willingness he had to let us run with it. After all, he didn't know us from Adam. However, we were also thrilled—and were 100 percent ready to take him up on his offer.

We flew back from Denver and immediately sent Andrew a proposal. We worried that if we waited too long he'd probably change his mind. But he got the proposal, told us it was great, and then gave us the keys to the business.

The story of how we became involved emphasizes the principles of trust and empowerment, which were the foundation of Startup Weekend from the beginning. Andrew decided to trust two young guys who just showed up on his doorstep one day. He didn't know us well. But his attitude on his method was, "If these guys do a good job, great. If not, I can always take it back from them."

It then quickly became a question of whom *we* could trust. As two guys who were trying to build something, we realized that Startup Weekend could only be successful if we did it on a large scale. We didn't pay ourselves for six months. We were living in a condo together and were absolutely broke. We knew that the key to getting support for the enterprise was to expand it—but how? We couldn't do it by managing every event ourselves. Not only was that logistically difficult, but we also didn't know every city well enough to get the right people to show up.

Should we really be responsible for the entire event budget and all logistics, everything from A to Z? Yes, we might make more money personally; but it would be a significantly higher amount of work and the events wouldn't turn out as well.

At the first Startup Weekend we hosted in San Francisco, California, Franck showed up. He heard about our endeavor from a friend and had just flown in from Paris that day. He was completely exhausted, but he loved the atmosphere. He had been involved in startups himself and had an engineering background. So by the end of Friday night, he had convinced us that he should host an event in France. Who would have thought?

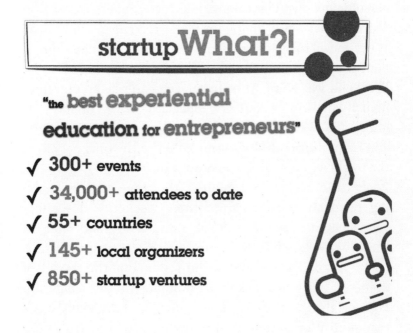

startup **What?!**

"the best experiential education for entrepreneurs"

✓ **300+** events
✓ **34,000+** attendees to date
✓ **55+** countries
✓ **145+** local organizers
✓ **850+** startup ventures

Franck Nouyrigat

In 2008 I did a one-year world tour with the goal of finding the best place to launch my new startup venture (I ended up choosing the United States). After my world trip, I spent six months saving money in order to be able to launch. When I met Marc in San Francisco in 2009, I was working on an iPhone application that went on to raise micro-venture capital. I met Clint later on, in France, and we became very good friends. A month after working for fun with Marc and Clint on Startup Weekend strategies I ended up in Seattle, Washington. This was where I made the decision of a lifetime. Marc, Clint, and I were the perfect team and we were working 24 hours a day on Startup Weekend. But Startup Weekend was very fragile. I made the decision to jump off the cliff with them—instead of pursuing my own ideas alone, I decided to make a donation of the money I was saving for my own company to Startup Weekend. This gave my family and friends some doubts, but I was completely confident. I had no doubt that Startup Weekend was going to be huge. You can't be an entrepreneur if you don't take risks, especially when the future is uncertain. While I realize how lucky I was to meet Marc and Clint as friends, I also think they're the only people in the world with whom I would want to work.

For the first several months, the three of us were flying everywhere to organize these weekends. I spent a year sleeping on one side of a couch and working on the other side while Marc and Clint were working furiously on the other side of the room. But the model of doing it ourselves wasn't sustainable in the long run. For one thing, we didn't know enough about every city's community of potential entrepreneurs to run truly successful events everywhere. One of the important features of Startup Weekend is that it can adapt to the culture around it. If a city is more traditional, Startup Weekend will provide formal nametags or slightly different food. But you have to know a particular place's culture in order to realize who should be there and how to make the participants most comfortable.

Marc, Clint, and I knew we were going to have to trust other people who were familiar with specific locations in order to guide the operation as we expanded to new locations. We relied on volunteers on the ground to help us, many of whom had previously participated in a Startup Weekend and wanted to bring it to their own hometowns. The whole enterprise grew organically to the point where now we were getting several e-mails a week from people asking if they could host a Startup Weekend themselves.

The first of these individuals was Shane Reiser, who wanted to organize a Startup Weekend in Des Moines, Iowa. That was an interesting experiment for Startup Weekend. In cities like San Francisco or Seattle, you know you have a built-in group of young, dynamic entrepreneurs, people who are used to the idea of startups. But how would this work in a mid-sized town in Middle America? *Would* it work? We had our doubts.

But Shane knew better. He had moved to Des Moines in 2009, and was going to some Tweetups (meetups for people on Twitter). He always saw a handful of budding entrepreneurs in the corner at these events, talking to each other about their ideas. But Shane was frustrated. Why weren't they *doing* anything—like taking the lead and actually starting companies? They had plenty of cool ideas but they were fearful. They didn't know how to get started, and they didn't know the right people. When Shane read about Startup Weekend, he sensed it would be a great motivator for the sidelined entrepreneurs.

Startup Weekend has hosted events in over 200 cities in more than 60 countries—none of which would have been possible unless we, the organization's leaders, trusted people on the ground to run these events well. We allow almost anyone to be a local organizer. Yes, we have an application process; but all we really want to see is that applicants truly care about the community, and that there is no other reason behind their desire to host an event.

Generally, it's a good indicator if someone is reaching out to you. It's almost like when you're dating someone who tells you, "I like you." It doesn't mean that you'll be the perfect match in the end, but you might at least want to consider that this person has something to offer. People who claim to want to host a Startup Weekend have heard about us, and tell us that they want to subscribe to our philosophy. So that's an automatic point in their favor.

Shane was a little surprised by our attitude. As he says, "Marc, Clint, and Franck didn't make me videotape myself. They didn't make me take a test or anything. They just asked me what I needed to know and then they sent me to New York."

Jon Rossi, who now leads Startup Weekend Denver, was also taken aback by the trust we placed in him. He marvels about the fact that he was able to represent our organization at an event in Denver without having ever met any member of our staff. The feeling of empowerment was particularly important to him. "With all the distrust in the world today, I was shocked that I didn't have to jump over hurdles, fill out lengthy forms, give a sample of my DNA, sign a Truth-in-Lending Act document, or take a polygraph in front of retired KGB officer." Jon has also embraced our attitude in his dealings with Startup Weekend activities—as well as the rest of his work life. "Ever since attending my first Startup Weekend in 2010, I have taken the philosophy of 'trust first, doubt later and only if given cause' and tried to implement it with the people I do work with on a daily basis."

Make no mistake—we have certainly had organizers who have botched things up, and about whom we've received some negative feedback. But business, especially startup business, is about taking risks. If we don't take a chance on people, the likelihood is that we'll never get anything off the ground in a lot of cities where we currently operate.

Startup Weekend has an internal wiki with documents full of advice to help guide new organizers through the process. We give them this, and then we say, "Run with it." We want to empower them to be their own evangelists in the community for Startup Weekend, and we don't want to get in the way of their doing what is best for their community. If we decide to go ahead with a new volunteer, we'll give them all of our materials, an e-mail address at Startup Weekend, and have our designers put together a logo to help them advertise their event.

How We Empower People to Get the Most Out of Startup Weekend

There is a very low barrier to entering a Startup Weekend as a participant. The cost for a weekend is under $100, and that includes food and all the coffee you can drink. Sure, you might get a few people who come for the muffins; but they quickly realize there are easier ways to get a free breakfast. We recognize that there are people in all different fields who may want to participate, and people from all walks of life who have ideas. And we don't want to discourage anyone from coming. We have to take a leap of faith. And we have to encourage others to take a leap of faith as well. One woman named Carmen e-mailed Shane about one of the first events he was hosting. Though she thought the event sounded cool, she worried that her skills wouldn't be very valuable to the other participants. She had done some script writing for children's television shows and couldn't see how that was going to fit in with a startup business. She knew she was a good writer and a creative

thinker, but she had never thought of herself as an entrepreneur before.

> ## Do you consider yourself to be an entrepreneur?
>
> While the news is full of stories of business
> geniuses and technology gurus who build
> multimillion-dollar companies seemingly
> overnight, being an entrepreneur is a journey.
> Do you see a problem and have an idea for an
> innovative solution? Be it in the realm of the
> arts, education, engineering, health care, and
> beyond, your desire to create change makes
> you an entrepreneur.

Shane could tell that Carmen wasn't very confident, so
he wrote her back encouraging her to come anyway:
"Clearly, you're interested in entrepreneurship and you
reached out to me for a reason. I guarantee your skills will
be valuable."

Shane didn't see Carmen much over the weekend.
She did pitch an idea Friday night, but it didn't get
enough interest to get off the ground. However, when
Sunday rolled around, Shane saw Carmen on stage giving the presentation for her team. Shane said he was
pretty surprised: One of the things she had said in her
e-mail was that she was a bad public speaker and was
embarrassed to get on stage in front of people. But
according to Shane, "She rocked it. She got up on
stage, and you could tell she was super excited to be on
this team with these people, [with whom] she had
developed [some solid] relationships."

After the event, Carmen came up to Shane and hugged him with tears in her eyes. She told him Startup Weekend had been "a life-changing experience," and said, "I don't know if this team is going continue, but whether it does or not, I'm definitely interested in entrepreneurship now. You've opened my eyes to this world of technology and entrepreneurship, and I've met some amazing people."

Carmen didn't have this life-changing experience because someone lectured her on the principles of entrepreneurship or told her how to start a company. While there are some formal presentations at Startup Weekend by entrepreneurs and business leaders who know something about entrepreneurship, attendance at these lectures is far from mandatory. We know that if people think their time is better spent working on their project than listening to an expert, then they should work on their projects. We recognize that people have sacrificed their free time to be at these events. They're not kids in school; they're grown-ups with full-time jobs and bills to pay. And learning at Startup Weekend happens because of the work that they do—not because they're sitting back and passively listening to others talk.

Why You Have to Have Trust to Be a Successful Entrepreneur

People come to Startup Weekends for different reasons. Some have a business idea already in mind, and they see Startup Weekend as a vehicle for making that idea succeed. However, this can be difficult at times. What if you assemble a team and the people on it like your idea, or a part of your idea, but envision it playing out in a different way? Part of being an active and valuable participant at Startup Weekend is making sure that you trust your partners and that you empower them to make decisions about your idea.

The only teams that will be really successful are those who discuss an idea at an early enough stage. The idea should be sufficiently undeveloped, and have a founder who hasn't yet decided exactly how it should be executed. The earlier that people are willing to get input, the more likely they are to have a successful venture.

For many people, though, Startup Weekend's value lies much more in the relationships that they form at our events than in the business ideas themselves. People will leverage those relationships after Startup Weekend has ended in order to form new companies and gain new contacts in the business world.

Researchers Friederike Welter and David Smallbone write in an *Entrepreneur* article that while the role of trust in entrepreneurship is not fully understood yet, one beneficial effect may be that "Not all business relationships need to be regulated via contracts, thus allowing [the entrepreneur] to reduce transaction costs." Trust, in other words, can simplify matters and make business work more smoothly. We have certainly found that to be the case.

However, we don't establish trust with others in a vacuum; and researchers have found that trust is not simply bilateral. It also depends on the norms and rules of the environment that surround the people who are forming a relationship. And this is even *more* important for entrepreneurs than it is for established businesses. As Welter and Smallbone explain, "Entrepreneurs are more likely to find themselves in a bootstrapping situation where they have to develop an identity as a trustworthy person." In other words, trust is so important at Startup Weekend because Startup Weekend is a *community*. And even people who are in the first hour of their first weekend of participation become integrated in that community.

> Have you experienced the power of early and inherent trust? When you knew someone trusted you, did you feel empowered to competently execute tasks? Have you ever empowered someone else by giving them your full trust? What were the results?

In some places, of course, this culture of trust comes a bit more slowly. As one Startup Weekend facilitator told us, "In Singapore, sharing one's most inner thoughts has always been an issue, especially with a room full of strangers." Still, though, he says that the environment Startup Weekend creates can encourage even the most reticent types to express themselves. "Once [participants begin to share] . . . ideas and thoughts on a trusted stage, the best ideas will arise with passionate supporters and more projects will be taken forward to actual launch."

One of Startup Weekend's greatest advantages is that it is local. Therefore, there's a good chance that those attending may have seen, worked with, or know someone who knows the other people there. This breaks down the barriers a bit. It is easy to imagine how another organization might just decide that everyone should fly to San Francisco for the weekend, thinking that just being near Silicon Valley will get everyone in the right mood. However, from our perspective, that would defeat the purpose. We want Startup Weekend to put down roots in each community, to help local people build locally, and perhaps even solve community problems.

Some might assume that nowadays, in this digital information/social networking age, people no longer need to sit next to those with whom they're working. After all, can't everyone just work from home and communicate online? Isn't it just easier—and more comfortable—to stay in your pajamas anyway? Well, you can take that approach; however, many entrepreneurs find it doesn't work as well as they'd like. This is why people from different startups have begun using shared workspaces, and going to places like coffee shops. As it turns out, that face-to-face contact is crucial not only to developing great ideas but for building trust as well.

While we always encourage people to trust others they meet at Startup Weekend from the get-go, we also know that the trust can't remain blind for long. Danielle Morrill, a veteran participant of Startup Weekends and startup companies, says that she loves being able to reach out to other Startup Weekend alums in different parts of the country and around the world. She'll send out an e-mail: "I'm coming to Chicago and I'd really like to meet some developers and entrepreneurs in your community. Can you connect me?"

What makes the Startup Weekend network so powerful? Danielle explains, "You don't stay in the network unless you actually *get stuff done*. It's pretty awesome to have that kind of access to smart people who [are actually accomplishing something]." In fact, she says, "I imagine [that] if my company got really big someday, [Startup Weekend] would be the most efficient way for me to hire people." The Startup Weekend brand has become synonymous with people who are willing to do the work. When people approach others they have met at our events, they trust that the work will get done.

That spirit of trust and community also pervades many of the innovations that come out of the weekends. For example, at a Startup Weekend in Brazil, someone suggested a mobile application that listed the Saõ Paulo bus schedules. We, too, were a little surprised to find that there were no schedules posted at the bus stops. People stand 20 yards behind the bus to see what number it is; then they sprint to the stop to make it onboard when it arrives. This is obviously a weakness in local government and infrastructure, but one that became solvable when a group of willing and able participants got together. In addition to posting schedules in a way that is accessible by mobile phone, the participants also worked to develop a network of people who would make sure that the buses have numbers on them, and that the schedules were correct.

These Startup Weekend participants are building on the trusting relationships they have developed and trying to bring that level of trust—a real working relationship—into their larger communities. After the recent devastating earthquake and tsunami in Japan, folks at a Startup Weekend in Cambridge, England, set up a humanitarian website for the victims to find cherished lost belongings. While local relief efforts saved lives and addressed immediate needs, the team at Cambridge developed a tool for a later stage when victims want to find lost belongings that have sentimental value. BelongingsFinder.org (in Japanese: Monosagashi.org) will help to restore identity by enabling people to photograph, upload, and search details of lost belongings. This free-of-charge application can be used by relief organizations, individuals, governments, and local communities.

One of the founders, a University of Cambridge student named Stefano Orowitsch, wrote to us that there was "no way I could have ignored Friday's news during this year's Startup Weekend. I immediately decided to team up with some of the world's best software engineers and mentors at Cambridge Startup Weekend." Indeed, by the end of the weekend, Orowitsch's team had developed Belongings-Finder.org. He wanted to "create hope for victims who lost their belongings." Users of the site are able to upload pictures of any object they find to a database via a mobile app, while others are able to search for missing objects on the website. Additionally, the whole service is being provided free of charge.

We read recently about something called the Legatum Prosperity Index—a global study that looks at the business climates in a variety of countries. We were not surprised to find that a country's ability to foster a climate of entrepreneurship has a significant effect on that country's overall well-being. An atmosphere of trust is at the heart of both.

It can be scary trying to be an entrepreneur. But we need to help people come together and move beyond that feeling. All you need are the right people and the right resources to begin creating solutions. Our philosophy is all about building trust in a community so that we can create the newest, greatest, and most innovative businesses imaginable.

Startup Weekend Co-directors in Seattle (L–R): Nouyrigat, Nelsen, and Nager.

1

No Talk, All Action
Action-Based Networking

LET'S SAY YOU'RE new to a city and you want to start dating. Where do you go to begin? Do you walk into a bar, sit down, and just hope that Mr. or Ms. Right will plop themselves down next to you and strike up a conversation? Probably not. After all, you could be there for years. And, let's face it—you might be drunk by the time your true love showed up anyway. Any number of people may come in while you're waiting, but you won't know anything about them and they won't know anything about you. So, aside from the assumptions you can make about the way they dress or what they're drinking, you'd be starting from scratch. Even after a brief conversation, you still probably won't know a lot more. These kinds of interactions are, almost by definition, superficial.

For years, advice columnists have told us that if we want to meet people, we should go *do something*. If we join a running club, we'll meet people with whom we at least have running in common. If we volunteer for Habitat for Humanity, we'll find people who are interested in public service and maybe like working with their hands. If we join a book club . . . well, you get the idea.

The advice that's traditionally been given to lonely hearts is even truer for budding entrepreneurs. You cannot simply wait for the right people to walk into your life or even walk into your office. You have to go out and *do* something to find them. And you have to do something *with* them in order to find out if you've got the right match.

So what are the options? A lot of people try business school. In fact, record numbers of individuals are applying to MBA programs these days. And no wonder; business school allows you to work with other students on projects and see where their talents lie, what interests them, how they work under pressure, and so on. You can stay up late into the night preparing for classes. People's true colors come out. And when you graduate, you have a built-in alumni network to draw on for your later career.

But business school is a big investment. Moreover, getting an MBA takes a lot of time—and time is one thing that entrepreneurs don't have. If you have an idea for a company now—or if what really gets you going in the morning is putting a startup idea in motion—then having to wait around to complete the business school cycle is not for you. Given the need to take the GMAT and undergo the application process, it will most likely be more than a year before you can even get in.

Finally, when it comes to meeting the right people with the right skills for what you want to do right now, business school might not cut it. You may have had good, smart people in your graduating class 10 years ago, but have they kept up? Are they the best developers or the best marketers today? Really, who knows what—and who—they know?

We have also been told that networking in an MBA program is not all it's cracked up to be. Candidates are expected to attend networking events as part of the MBA program. However, most of these events, though technically "professional," are centered on golf tournaments, picnics, or barbecues. At almost all of them, the emphasis is on talking rather than learning or doing. The more casual events stress the importance of listening to more experienced people talk about their life stories and best practices (many of which are not even relevant today). It can be a very didactic, top-down approach to information sharing.

One Startup Weekend participant told us that while she certainly made some good connections at these

B-school events, "most were lost opportunities in the sense that it was extremely difficult to actually witness the capabilities and skills of the people I was supposed to be meeting. I found a few good mentors, but was continually frustrated by how hard it was to get to know fellow MBA candidates." She said that the networking events were either designed to resemble cocktail hours—situations where "you only skim the surface with new people or stick to people you already know."

None of this is meant to knock business school. It is still a place where you may gain important skills for your career. However, it's simply to say that getting an advanced degree may not be the most efficient route for meeting startup cofounders.

So what about networking on your own—attending functions at a company where you already work, or seeking out other people in your area who might be interested in entrepreneurship?

This can certainly be a helpful career move; there's no telling whom you will find by putting out some feelers at local business or social events. But that's exactly the problem: There's no telling whom you will find. Think about what you would say to someone you just met about your own business credentials. Would you recite your resume? Find the perfect anecdote to illustrate your skills? Can you drop the name of the right mutual acquaintance? Maybe—maybe not. Maybe you will bond over the fact that your brother went to the same college as this person's sister. But sooner or later, it becomes a lot like trying to find dates on a barstool. What can you find out about the other person and what can he or she find out about you?

Now, think about the business cards you collect at other networking events. Can you even remember which person was which by the time you get home?

Making the right impression on other people at a golf tournament can be an important skill. But it's not important for everyone. For someone in public relations, it's a vital part of the job. But what difference would this make for a developer or a designer or an engineer? As one veteran of a number of startups in the Seattle area likes to say, "Tech folks are not natural networkers." And we don't think they should have to be.

What other people ultimately care about—and really, *should* care about—is the quality of your work. But you can't whip out your laptop (or even your iPad) and, while holding your white wine in one hand and balancing your hors d'oeuvres on your knee, proceed to show someone how you work.

For that, you need to apply the action-based networking principles of Startup Weekend.

You *Must* Join a Team

We at Startup Weekend don't have much in the way of wine or those fancy little quiches. However, by the end of the weekend you will truly understand the skill sets of the people around you—and they will understand yours.

From the easy registration method to the informal Friday night dinner, attendees are expected to talk to one another; and since the only thing they have in common (up until that point) is an interest in entrepreneurship, it is easy to learn about their peers' dreams, ideas, strengths, and weaknesses. When you know that you are supposed to join a team with strangers and work together all weekend, the pressure is on to get to know everyone in the room and to find out what sort of talents surround you.

- Think about the last professional networking event you attended: How many lasting connections did you make?
- Now, think about the last time you participated in an "extra-curricular" group event: How many lasting connections did you make?
- Most likely, your shared interests led to stronger connections and more lasting ties. If you want to begin work on your startup idea, surround yourself with other people who are hoping to do the same!

Friday night is especially intense, because it's when the team creation happens. Yet, even the long working days of Saturday and Sunday provide ample opportunities to create, build, collaborate, explore, and brainstorm—not only with the members of one's team, but also with other attendees.

One Startup Weekend participant recalls an event in Vancouver, British Columbia, where teams were required to check in every so often with the entire group. She recounts, "Although it was hard to stop frantically working on our own projects, I loved hearing about what other teams were building and their calls for help. It was so empowering to see [the] brilliant developers, designers, marketers, and project managers that we had in the room . . . it gave me a great excuse to walk up to someone new at Saturday dinner and ask them more about their graphic design experiences."

Because Startup Weekends combine the dual requirements of teamwork and *proof of concept*, people feel

motivated to show off what they can do and find out what
everyone else in the room is capable of. It's fine for someone to brag that they are the world's best developer or a
marketing guru. However, when you watch how five other
people work together and see the quality of their output for
yourself, you build a foundation for future relationships
or networks that is so much stronger than the tenuous
(and occasionally, meaningless) exchange of business cards
at a bar.

We have also found that it is easy for budding entrepreneurs to become cynical. After a while, you can meet a certain number of people who say they can do things but then
don't follow through. Many entrepreneurs begin to feel as if
they should just go it alone. They assume that others don't
share their energy or passion, or don't have the right skill
set. One Startup Weekend attendee named Mike Vandenbos describes how he has been an entrepreneur since the
age of four—when he started selling flower seeds with his
older brother, making a three-cent commission on each
pack. When he got a little older and more ambitious, he
became a paper boy and then started a small engine-repair
shop while he was in high school. After that, he began a
golf event consulting business.

Looking back, Mike says, his one glaring shortcoming
was always his "desire to go it alone"—no more partnerships with the older brother or anyone else. As an adult trying to launch new ventures, Mike realized that the stakes
are much higher. He has learned through Startup Weekend
that he can "walk with other entrepreneurs."

Other Startup Weekend participants are well aware
that they need partners, but they often don't know where
to find them. Jesse Maddox learned what a good networking tool Startup Weekend can be when he returned from a
trip to Vietnam with an idea for an application to help

tourists communicate with locals. He recalled watching the exchanges between the two groups and cringing: "Usually when a fruit seller approaches a tourist, the tourist sees him coming and goes into what I call 'No mode.' He shakes his head at the fruit seller, saying 'no' over and over, and ends up either erupting in frustration or simply ignoring the person." Needless to say, the entire exchange is a disaster for both parties.

Maddox remembers that after taking a few language lessons with a couple of locals, he was finally able to communicate effectively and politely, thereby avoiding the embarrassing exchange described above. "When the fruit seller approached, I smiled and said 'No rồi' (pronounced 'naw zoi')—I'm full already." Maddox was excited when a huge grin came over the vendor's face; then she laughed and said something back, which he didn't understand. "It didn't matter. In just two short syllables, I'd avoided an awkward situation, engaged positively with the local culture, and had a memorable experience myself."

Maddox came back to his home in Atlanta, Georgia, a few months later with a business plan in hand for helping foreigners learn key local phrases very quickly. The program would include phrases designed for different types of travelers—businessmen, tourists, and so on. One would even offer instruction on flirting in a foreign language. Maddox sent out the idea to a number of friends and acquaintances in the hopes of securing funding. But he heard the same response over and over: Great idea, but we can't offer you any funding until we see that you've put a team together.

"To me, this seemed like the classic chicken-and-egg problem. I couldn't get a team without investment, and I couldn't get investment without a team," Maddox says. His experience illustrates what we think of as one of the biggest myths about entrepreneurship—that finding capital is the biggest hurdle to putting together a successful venture. However, as Maddox found, the capital was available, but the investors cared about the people. They wanted to know who was going to be on the team. After all, how could they know that this group of people was skilled enough and could work well together if Maddox didn't even know who was going to be working with him?

Finally, one entrepreneur-turned-angel investor suggested that he attend a Startup Weekend to find a team of people.

Maddox managed to get into Atlanta's Startup Weekend at the last minute, only because one of the other weekend participants dropped out—something he now calls a very lucky break. He pitched his "Triplingo" idea (as he called his business) on Friday night, and it was a hit. In fact, it was chosen as one of the top 12 ideas pitched that night. Maddox easily found nine people to work on his team—including a designer, programmers who could work on both web and mobile applications, and marketing talent. As Maddox fondly recalls, "Our team composition allowed us to break our work into different modules. It meant that there was never a point where we had people sitting around with nothing to do."

Maddox acknowledges that his plan was very ambitious. By the end of the weekend, he wanted a functioning prototype of both the web and iPhone app. To accomplish this in one weekend, the team he attracted to his idea would not only have to be extremely talented; they would have to be highly motivated as well. The group worked through some difficult problems; for example, a bug in the server program they were using held up their progress for several hours, and they were preparing their presentation until the last possible moment. But it paid off in the end. Triplingo was voted the winner of Startup Weekend Atlanta and it had seed funding to get off the ground within two days. Both CNN and the *Atlanta Journal Constitution* subsequently ran pieces on the company.

Maddox reflects that, "Without Startup Weekend, it might never have happened. Our team would have never formed; I might still be wandering the streets of Atlanta looking for cofounders, and we'd never have our chance to change the way the world travels." The story of Triplingo illustrates how important it is to create your own team—to get out there and find the right people, and don't wait for them to find you. Otherwise, you'll be on that barstool alone all night.

The Triplingo team's tremendous sense of motivation is not unique. People come to Startup Weekend ready to work. They have set aside this time—away from their jobs, their families, and all of the demands that usually grab our attention. Knowing that the Sunday night deadline is fast approaching turns people into real workhorses.

Tyler Koblasa, the founder of Ming.ly, an application that helps people manage their professional networking, says that he found the perfect team at a Startup Weekend: two Google engineers, a former Hulu vice president, a Georgetown MBA, and a lawyer who also did design work. But it was not just the talent assembled at the meeting that made it such a perfect mix for Koblasa. He might have encountered them all somewhere else, "but they wouldn't have been in a room ready to work." Tyler says that his team had "a super-charged, 'we want to win' attitude."

Breaking Down Barriers

Action-based networking does more than provide entrepreneurs with team members quickly and efficiently. It also

breaks down a lot of the artificial barriers that stand between entrepreneurs. Meeting potential business partners
through the traditional routes can mean picking people
who look like us, or went to the same schools, or come
from the same part of the country or the world. However,
we all know that these are arbitrary reasons to hire someone or work with someone.

In a setting like the one presented at Startup Weekend,
entrepreneurs use the people who are there. They can't sit
around and wait for someone they feel comfortable with in
a social situation. They have to find someone they can *work*
with, and the sooner, the better.

At Startup Weekend, they get a chance to see *how* people really work, regardless of their backgrounds. For people
who may be nervous about working with someone with different personal or professional experience, the action-based
networking can also provide a kind of low-risk way of trying
it out. As one startup veteran explained to us, building a
relationship with a cofounder is like getting into a marriage. You will have to spend long hours with this other
person, probably in small, enclosed spaces. Each person's
hopes, dreams, and finances will be intertwined with
the other person's. Once you get the startup off the ground,
it will be hard to get out of the relationship if it doesn't
work out.

Startup Weekend is essentially a chance to give this
marriage a spin before actually tying the knot. Those 54
hours of work give you a chance to see whether things will
work out. And if they don't, nothing is lost. At the end of
the weekend, you can just walk away; after all, you haven't
bought the wedding gown or paid for the catering yet. As
one organizer told us, "By Saturday afternoon, if you realize
this person is driving you crazy, you know that it's all going
to be over by Sunday night—and you can just walk away."

Another Startup Weekend participant compared his experience to a camping trip he attended in high school designed to get kids socialized; because let's face it—in large groups of strangers, we all tend to act like we're in high school. He says, "Over the years, the teachers had developed a great solution to break down the social barriers: week one was training and prep, and then week two of school was a camping trip (which also satisfied our Phys Ed requirement!). We arrived not knowing each other, but after spending a week hiking, eating, sleeping (and doing everything else) in the woods, it became pretty much impossible to maintain any sort of distance." Looking back, he says, "Forty people won't necessarily all be friends, but we were all close after that week. In the same way, Startup Weekend throws a bunch of strangers together in the wilderness and forces them to work together, social norms be damned."

Another participant named Sasha Pasulka compares Startup Weekend to summer camp. "It's not that anyone [went] sailing, or made a lanyard, or got to second base with me before a counselor came around with a flashlight; but everyone in the room that night bonded intensely in a short period of time." She recalls, "By Saturday morning, I was not in a room full of strangers anymore. By Sunday evening, I was in a room with some of my closest friends in the city." Knowing very few people in the area before that Friday, Sasha says, her professional network "exploded," and "so did my grasp of up-and-coming technologies, markets, and potential teammates." Since that first Startup Weekend, she has worked as a columnist for a startup-focused website, sold a company she launched, and worked as a consultant for other ventures.

Putting people together in environments like the one at Startup Weekend serves a dual purpose. It is a way of mitigating future financial risk, since you'll find out early if your fellow participants are capable of helping you start a venture. It's also a method of ensuring that the startup experience is personally fulfilling. Since 90 percent of start-ups fail, part of the payoff has to be experience. If you don't enjoy working with your partners, then that experience is bound to be a bad one. If you've worked with them for a weekend, you're in much better shape to evaluate whether you'll have fun working with them in the long term. A few participants build companies that succeed and grow beyond Startup Weekend, and almost every participant finds working relationships, friendships, and sometimes even a cofounder at Startup Weekend.

Taking Advantage of High-Energy, Low-Risk Settings

The low-risk nature of networking at Startup Weekend prompts many people to decide that they can safely expand their horizons in other ways as well. Kyle Kesterson was a toy developer living in Seattle, who didn't think he had anything to learn from Startup Weekend. According to Kesterson, friend and startup veteran Donald DeSantis "described it to me as working with people on building iPhone and web apps and how cool it was, which I just kind of let graze my ears but not sink in too far." Kesterson remembers DeSantis's efforts to convince him to go to a Startup Weekend event: "I made up all sorts of excuses and ended up missing Friday night altogether, thinking I was just going to bail on the whole weekend."

At 1 AM on Saturday, Kesterson remembers getting a call from DeSantis, "sounding like he just outran the cops or something." DeSantis reported that the Startup Weekend experience was amazing but that there were "*no* designers there and that it didn't matter what my background was; if I had *any* design skills or eye for aesthetic, I'd be in high demand." DeSantis would not take no for an answer.

So, Saturday morning at 7:30 AM, Kesterson arrived at his first Startup Weekend. He acknowledges that the project he ended up working on sounds a little ridiculous: a virtual pet created to look like John Stamos. This *Tamagotchi*, as this type of digital creature is called, was supposed to be a kind of nostalgia item for people who remember Stamos as Uncle Jesse on the 1980s sitcom *Full House*.

Kesterson remembers sketching the creature and then working on its various features on his computer. Everyone else was working on coding or PowerPoint presentations, so most people would walk by his laptop and be a little surprised.

However, many people were also amused and impressed. By the end of the weekend, Kesterson had a pile of business cards, and a couple of job offers. One person even offered to give his portfolio to the director of creative development at Pixar.

Kesterson's team won the award for business idea most likely to make a million dollars—and to this day, people who attended that weekend still talk about it. More importantly, Kyle had his first taste of life in the startup world. Now, he is the cofounder of a startup called Giant Thinkwell, which builds fan engagement platforms for celebrities and influencers to grow, engage, and monetize their followings through online and mobile experiences. They've moved on from John Stamos to the likes of Lady Gaga. Kesterson is also a graduate of Seattle's TechStars program, an initiative that supports entrepreneurs who demonstrate promise.

Looking back on his experience, Kesterson says, "Starting Giant Thinkwell wasn't even a thought trying to form in my head" before Startup Weekend. He admits that

"I had absolutely no network, insight, or understanding of the startup/tech world. Even if I was motivated to start a company that [went anywhere] beyond my freelance design and illustration, I wouldn't have the first clue on how to put together an investor pitch deck, who to talk to, what to take into account when forming a team. I was absolutely green, naïve, and alone."

{ Just like you used to write rough drafts of papers in school, spending meaningful time on a startup rough draft isn't a waste of time. Creating "rough drafts" at high-energy, low-risk collaborative events helps identify and strengthen weaknesses. Think of it as a dress rehearsal for your startup! }

The action-based networking that he found at Startup Weekend provided Kesterson with not only a great list of new contacts and a lot more knowledge of the startup world; it also placed him in an energetic world of motivated people. "Startup Weekend was like a *Pulp Fiction* shot of adrenaline to the heart," he says. As a character designer, he can't resist a cartoon comparison; and he says he felt the same way Little Foot did in *The Land Before Time* when he finally made it to the Great Valley. Kesterson explains: "It instantly made my previous world feel so primitive and out of the loop. People at Startup Weekend were so high on the rush of creativity and productivity and eager to collaborate."

Getting the chance to meet all of these people from other fields was something that Kesterson says didn't happen for him in school or in his day job as a toy designer. Startup Weekend introduced him to "people on one end of the spectrum from Microsoft and Google," as well as to those whom Kyle thinks of as being from a "sterile business-to-business environment." He explains that while he doesn't really fit into that world either, the people who came from those other types of environments "had really interesting ideas about what collaboration with someone with my skill set could look like."

In fact, many of the people who attend Startup Weekends work at larger companies. While they may feel as though they have unlimited resources where they are, that can be paralyzing in a way—because they start to believe that they need all those resources in order to start up a new company. But they don't. That's exactly why it can be very beneficial for them to network with veterans of startups and work alongside people who have the courage to engage in this process.

Kesterson found people at Startup Weekend who were highly polished, and some who were not; he found people who were into social gaming and some who were definitely not. "It was just this huge array, but it all had to do with technology and flourishing ideas. And everyone is really excited and really open and generous with their ideas." He says that this kind of openness is something he hadn't encountered before. "This wasn't heavily guarded brilliance"; this was people "just wanting to get as much feedback as they can and really digging. And that digging included finding out what ideas you might have."

Kesterson says that when he was in school, he imagined that some day he might be successful enough to become a freelance designer, but even in that case, he would just be working out the designs for someone else's ideas. He never dreamed that he could have his own company where he came up with the concepts for what he was designing, too.

Kesterson's educational experience prior to coming to Startup Weekend (which, if anything, was strictly limited to his talents) is not unique—and this is not only an American educational phenomenon. Thibaut Labarre, another Startup Weekend participant, explains that in his experience at the French *Grand Ecoles d'Ingénieurs*, "which are supposed to teach the best and brightest scientists and engineers," he was not exposed to people from other fields or people who had great entrepreneurial ideas. However, at a Paris Startup Weekend, Labarre and his team developed a website where people could share their insights about what was going to happen in the future. "The goal," he explains, "was to bring all brains together in order to have the best forecasts about what is going to happen." Labarre says he would like to make a course modeled on Startup Weekend a part of the curriculum at his university. "Startup Weekend gave me the startup spirit and the feeling that anything is possible when people from different backgrounds work together for a common cause."

Get Out of Your Bubble

Entrepreneurs have to be different from people who work for large companies. They can't just sit in their cubicle and interact with other people who do exactly what they do or have the same training they do. As a startup veteran and evangelizer for entrepreneurial networking, Bob Crimmins points out, "The most important relationships you have as an entrepreneur are with people who *don't* do what you do."

Entrepreneurs have to act like CEOs, only with a more hands-on approach. They have to know a little bit about every aspect of business. It's not that they have to be able to step in for the coders if the coders call in sick that day, but they do have to know what is involved in coding. They must develop a sense of how long things take and how the work gets done. However, our day-to-day interactions often don't provide us with the opportunity to see how our colleagues in other departments do their work. Getting out of the bubble of your own field is critical to being a successful entrepreneur. As we discuss later, Startup Weekend has allowed entrepreneurs to be able to look at the entire workflow and see how the whole process can be made better and more efficient.

Many of the project leaders at Startup Weekend like to be modest and say they just bought the coffee in the morning and the beer at night and it was really their team that did all the work. However, that's rarely the case. Keeping the team on an even keel, matching up individual skills with a particular element of the project, and ensuring that people are getting along and having fun while work is accomplished are important parts of being a startup founder. And the action-based networking at Startup Weekend gives budding entrepreneurs a chance to try out these roles.

And not all of the networking that happens is with your own team, either. One Startup Weekend participant, Alexa Andrzejewski, founded a company called Foodspotting, a social networking application that allows users to post pictures of and recommend their favorite dishes (not just their favorite restaurants.) Alexa describes how she came to the event with an idea in mind but didn't plan to fully develop it that weekend. Instead, she claimed a section of a blank wall and started to put up post-it notes with her team members that had design ideas written all over them. As Andrzejewski explains, "We wanted to brainstorm in a really visible way." And it worked beautifully; other SW participants would walk by and ask questions or make suggestions. "We talked to someone who did market research about how we could do research with restaurants to help Foodspotting [improve],

Half Baked

Half Baked is a great ice breaker that encourages Startup Weekend participants to relax, meet fellow attendees, practice pitching, and remember that we're all here to have fun. The half baked startup ideas encourage people to think creatively and can be adapted to many different situations.

1. Fill half a large whiteboard with all the random words you can think of: giraffe, banana, squishy, volcano, Big Foot, exploding, flying saucer, slippers, purple, Zeus, petunia . . .

2. Encourage the entire group to shout out more random words until the whiteboard is full.

3. Count off the group into roughly equal teams (six people per team seems to be the magic number). We like to divide people up so every seventh person is on the same team—that way even groups of friends are forced to split up and meet new people.

4. Each team has to choose two words from the board. These words are now the name of a startup. It's first come, first served for the word pairings and a word cannot be used twice. (For example, Team 4 chooses Exploding Banana so Team 7 must go from Squishy Banana to Squishy Slippers.)

5. Once they've chosen their words, the teams have 10 minutes to prepare a 1-minute presentation that explains their startup idea to the group (props and skits are welcome!).

6. In a random order, each team presents their brand new startup idea. Example: "We're Team 4 and we'd like to introduce you to Exploding Banana. We all know that kids don't always eat enough fruit and we feel that it's because fruit is boring. So how can parents make their kids want to eat fruit? By serving them safe but fun Exploding Bananas, of course! . . ."

7. The winning group is determined by the Applause-o-Meter and bragging rights are awarded.

*Startup Weekend would like to thank Dave McClure for introducing us to Half Baked.

and we talked to a lawyer who told us what's involved in actually starting up a company."

Andrzejewski got to pitch her idea over and over again to dozens of people, and receive valuable feedback along the way. By the time she left on Sunday, she had a much better idea of how to make her concept work effectively—and she had gotten *a lot* of practice selling the idea to potential users. Though Alexa didn't find the rest of her team at Startup Weekend, the connections she made there eventually granted her access to some initial funding for her venture.

Another Startup Weekend participant in Grand Rapids, Michigan, worked on a project called Rethink Water, which aims to reduce the waste created by plastic water bottles by installing water filtration machines on college campuses. He recalls of his teammates: "Our instant friendship, as well as their passion for the project and our common interests in bringing not only the Rethink Water project but other ideas on the table to market, served to fuel our energy throughout the weekend and to this day."

Like Alexa, this entrepreneur told us that it wasn't just the people on his own team who helped. "The collaborative and open nature of the weekend was an aspect I thoroughly enjoyed." He was impressed with the way "everyone was willing to share their work and help others with theirs. We could be wrestling with an issue one moment, when someone from another team would stop by, take a look, and offer other creative alternatives."

> There are many examples in everyday life when we rely on our friends' feedback: going shopping, choosing paint colors, planning a vacation, relationship advice—the list goes on and on. Given how important feedback is, don't neglect outside perspectives when building your startup!

Another woman came to Startup Weekend with the idea of doing something similar to Groupon, but gearing it solely toward women—that is, offering deals on products or services in which women would be interested. As with Groupon, the deal would only go through if enough people signed up for it. So, she assembled a team and sent out messages to all of the Startup Weekend participants asking for their feedback. They ended up changing their model during the course of the weekend to include the idea that a portion of the money was to be given to particular charities, and that they were going to let businesses keep a higher portion of the profits than Groupon gives them. It was a great business model by Sunday, but thanks to all the feedback they got from fellow Startup Weekend participants, it didn't look much like what they started with on Friday night.

If Not an Actual Startup, at Least Always Build Relationships

Startup Weekend has begun to attract investors and startup veterans to its events, people who want to see what (or, more importantly, who) is the *next big thing.* The world of startup funding can be complicated. Knowing the right people to ask, the right amount of money to ask for, pitching your idea correctly—these are all things about which someone just out of college or who has spent years working for a software firm might not have the slightest idea.

Investors are often bombarded with proposals for new business ideas. How can they know who will follow through? First-time entrepreneurs with no prior track record will have difficulty getting their proposals to the top of the pile. But Startup Weekend allows investors to watch the development of an idea from a pitch on Friday night (a twinkle in the founder's eye) to a real business model— and sometimes even a real business—by Sunday night. Even if an investor doesn't fund that idea, he may find a person he would be willing to back in the future.

Or, the reverse may occur. Danielle Siauw attended a Startup Weekend in Singapore where she pitched her idea for FashionSpace—basically, a site with racks of user-generated fashion magazines, a *Facebook for fashion* or a fashion aggregator and search engine rolled into one. As it turns out, her idea was not very popular among her fellow Startup Weekend participants and didn't get selected for further work. However, her pitch caught the attention of an angel investor. In short order, Siauw says, "I quit my dreary job and found new life in my new startup with the help of Startup Weekend. I am finally able to fulfill my dreams of being an entrepreneur."

Donald DeSantis, a veteran of a number of startups in the Seattle area, was attending a Startup Weekend in Costa Rica when he met one of the participants, a young man who had his own fledgling startup. Though it wasn't the project he ended up working on over the weekend, DeSantis proceeded to introduce the man to a number of the judges. The participant told them about his own business and eventually was promised some funding for it. As DeSantis relates, the man told him, "I didn't have any relationships with investors. In Costa Rica, it takes a long time to make those relationships, and there is a lot of red tape and greasing of palms. You just completely short-circuited the process for me."

Former Executive Director of the Northwest Entrepreneur Network, Rebecca Lovell has come to a number of Startup Weekends to offer the investor perspective. She recommends that Startup Weekend participants try to meet the judges and other guest speakers who are at the events. Lovell likens attending Startup Weekend to "having a passport that lasts a weekend. You need to take advantage of the time there to make strong connections." She says that many of the investors there are "naturally predisposed to help, but they're very, very busy." So, you have to make an impression on them during the weekend. You can't just hand someone your business card; you must engage them and create a genuine connection.

It helps that the judges and potential investors at Startup Weekend can see what participants are capable of doing—even if the idea that attendees work on over the weekend is not the one on which they ultimately hope to follow through. In fact, we think that budding entrepreneurs tend to be *too* focused on their actual ideas. We believe that it's the *people* who will make or break the venture, not the idea. As we said before, ideas are a dime a dozen. That is what makes the action-based networking at Startup Weekend so important. Those who attend will meet the people who can eventually determine a venture's success. Lovell also warns entrepreneurs against concentrating too much on their ideas, or thinking of Startup Weekend merely as a place to go to find people to do some free weekend work on their idea. "When people are married to an idea, it can go horribly wrong," she says.

One of our facilitators, who has worked with other startup mentorship programs like Y-Combinator, says that these types of programs pick companies to support based on the people who comprise the teams, and expect that the ideas will change along the way. "As a facilitator, I look for attendees on the sidelines Friday night who are struggling to figure out what team to join or [who] feel discouraged because their idea wasn't picked. I tell them to just talk to the teams and join one with people who seem fun."

Diversity of Backgrounds Is Key

Action-based networking is not only important to individual entrepreneurs; it's also vital to the process of establishing an infrastructure of startups in a particular place. In cities like New York or London, entrepreneurship may seem like old hat. But there are plenty of entrepreneurs around the country and the world who need an effective way of connecting with cofounders and colleagues—people who share that startup spirit. The kind of work that goes on at Startup Weekend allows people to form strong bonds that eventually grow into a community. Typically, Startup Weekend organizers have a lot of contacts in their startup, business, and/or tech communities. So, even though the barrier to entry may seem low, the events often turn out to be composed of a very highly motivated and connected group of participants.

And Startup Weekend's international outreach has meant that entrepreneurs looking to expand their horizons have a resource for finding like-minded people all over the globe. One Startup Weekend participant launched a company that provided beach lockers and electronic locker solutions in Portugal. She wanted to expand to France, but she realized she couldn't do it alone. So she came to a Startup Weekend in Toulouse and met "highly motivated people with diverse backgrounds" who helped her develop the plans for how to proceed in other countries.

The diversity of individual backgrounds is critical to Startup Weekend's success, and is necessary for assembling the right entrepreneurial teams. Eric Lagier is the founder of Memolane, a tool for collecting and organizing photos, music, video, tweets, status updates, and blogs—an all-in-one application. Of the two cofounders whom he met at a Startup Weekend in Copenhagen, he shares that one had very little in the way of formal education, while the other one had two masters' degrees. They were from different countries—his original team included people from Germany, the Netherlands, Sweden, the United Kingdom, and Denmark—and Eric is convinced that "under normal circumstances, we never would have met." He also marvels at the range of ages he found at Startup Weekend—from 20-year-olds to people who already had long careers in the corporate world under their belts.

At the very least, Eric says he could have spent six months trying to assemble not only a team with the right variety of skills but who also had a willingness to work with him on his project. "Those guys could have spent their weekend drinking and partying and whatnot. But they decided to spend it at Startup Weekend instead."

And it was not only his own team that came together like this; Eric has watched others, too. He speaks of one business development marketer who met a project manager with whom he created a successful startup. Looking back, Eric said that "a lot of energy was unleashed" when the two of them worked together.

Alexa Andrsejewski said she had a similar experience of finding a wide array of people at Startup Weekend. "I was a user-experience consultant," she says, "and I looked around at my network and realized that everyone I knew was also a user-experience person, which meant that all the people she knew could only fill one of the roles at Foodspotting. Alexa didn't know any investors or developers; as she half-jokes, "They go to developer camps, and things like that." One of the reasons she came to Startup Weekend was for "cross-pollination." Though Foodspotting didn't win the competition that weekend, one of the judges offered to give her team $5,000 after the competition was over—and subsequently provided a lot of advice about getting further funding.

How Do You Keep the Momentum Going?

One question we constantly ask ourselves is how to make Startup Weekend's atmosphere last in a community, even after the weekend is over. We don't think it's a coincidence that many of our participants are developing applications and programs that help people stay in touch and put like-minded people in contact with each other. The trend toward coworking spaces is an important development. The idea of people doing projects alongside each other, in person and in real time, will continue to encourage the kind of contact and action-based networking that begins at Startup Weekend.

When Tyler Koblasa noticed that something called "Coloft" opened up in Los Angeles, he suggested doing a Startup Weekend event there. "People know that they're going to be around this community and can find what they're looking for." Coworking spaces, he says, "are a critical component of catalyzing Startup Weekend because it becomes not just about those three days. It's about everything leading up to the event and what happens afterward." Tyler has even started sponsoring a monthly event there where people pay $10 to come work on a project from 7 PM to 2 AM for one evening with other attendees. "We want to [establish both] a feeder to Startup Weekend, and a support network afterward."

Action-based networking is an intensely local phenomenon. Not only do you need to be able to see people and talk to them; you need to be with them for hours, if not days, at a time. But that kind of local networking can also be expanded. There are people who come from out of town for our events and people who meet their cofounders and investors and colleagues through our extensive national and international network. You can take the knowledge you gain from other people at Startup Weekends and transform something local into something global.

For the past couple of years, a number of Startup Weekend team members have gone to the South by Southwest (SXSW) Festival in Austin, Texas. SXSW is not just a good place for us to meet energetic, independent-minded people. It's also an excellent model for Startup Weekend. If you think about it, people who make music or produce art or movies may attend cocktail parties or go to film school together. However, an event like SXSW or the Sundance Festival truly shows them what they are capable of doing. People come to those events with the knowledge that they will be able to see talent in action. The effects of

South by Southwest reverberate for the rest of the year in both the United States and in the global music industry.

As unique and intense as the Startup Weekend experience is, we also think it has broader, long-term implications. As people take the lessons of Startup Weekend and apply them in their own communities and spread them throughout a variety of places and industries, we hope they will become an integral part of an entrepreneurial revolution.

2

Good Ideas Need Great Teams
Pitch for Talent Not for Funding

IT'S FRIDAY NIGHT at 9 PM, and you're in a room packed with strangers. The boxes of pizza were emptied long ago and are now piled up in a corner, but a few people are still clutching (albeit warm) beers. It's loud in this Manhattan loft space. It's hot, too, and frankly, people are starting to smell a little. But you hardly notice. And you *definitely* don't make a move for the door. Instead, you try to carry on intense, vocal-cord-straining conversations about business ideas and computer coding, advertising and customer bases, venture capital and what entrepreneurial success looks like. You search, sometimes in vain, for the people you watched a few minutes ago trying to sell you their ideas. And you try to find people who are interested in your ideas. You are holding up pizza boxes with the name of your future company, writing with magic marker on the backs of paper plates and throwing them like Frisbees into the crowd—doing anything you can to make yourself stand out in this chaos.

Just a few minutes ago, there was some order in this room. You were patiently lined up along the wall with 30 other people, waiting to pitch an idea for a new business in 60 seconds. Even after 75 pitches, there was virtual silence when each person began to talk. When you looked over at the line snaking down the hall, you saw some people fidgeting, tucking in their shirts, and smoothing out their hair. Some were taking notes. Others were trying to memorize lines like they were auditioning for a Broadway play.

And you were asking yourself some questions, too: Should you try to be funny or serious? Who should you look at? Should you tell them about what you do during the rest of your life? Will anyone care? Should you mention how many other events like this you've come to? Will your accent be too heavy? Will you talk too loudly or not loudly enough? Sixty seconds, you begin to think, just isn't very long.

The Magic of 60 Seconds

When we set out to design the course of events at Startup Weekend, we didn't just pick 60 seconds arbitrarily to give people a hard time or because we like seeing that look of panic come over their faces when they notice the clock running out (though it is a little funny.) We wanted to be practical: No one would be able to go home on Friday night if we let all the people who wanted to pitch ideas go on any longer than that.

However, there was an even more important reason: 60 seconds is about the length of time you have in an elevator to explain the concept of your company to a total stranger (even less, if you get out on a lower floor). After that minute is up, you'll start to lose someone's attention. Even if you have a scheduled meeting with someone that's longer, the advice your seventh-grade teacher gave you is right: The topic sentence and the introductory paragraph need to be great. People will tune out if you can't grab their interest with the first few words that come out of your mouth.

So it's best to make those 60 seconds count. Here is the advice we give to participants in what we like to call "Friday Pitchfire" about the questions to answer in order to use their time wisely:

- 5 to 10 seconds: Who are you?
- 10 to 20 seconds: What's the problem your product/ service solves?
- 10 to 20 seconds: What's your solution?
- 5 to 10 seconds: Who do you need on your team?

I NEED + CONCLUSION

Anyone with a medical background is welcome; I need also a designer and anyone who wants or can do a mobile app. Let's save lives!

WHO YOU ARE

My name is Jen, I'm a Ruby on Rails developer, and I love cupcakes!

THE SOLUTION

I want to trace and geolocalize people who have prediabetic symptoms. Thus, we will build a real-time map. The aim is to communicate about this issue. I'm also planning to help people with prediabetes symptoms to get help, connecting them together using a mobile app.

THE PROBLEM

I wish I could help people with diabetes; currently there are more than 170 million people around the world suffering from diabetes. Prediabetes is the state in which some but not all of the diagnostic criteria for diabetes are met. It has been termed America's largest health care epidemic, affecting more than 57 million Americans.

It's been our experience that participants tend to focus too much on the first one: Who are you? When you're pitching an idea for a startup company, the audience *does* want to know something about you—if you have had experience in the field. For example, a guy who wanted to launch a company that would send kids a surprise toy in the mail each month said that he had worked in the toy industry, which of course gave him some credibility. But people at our events don't much care where you went to school, let alone if you finished. You can let the other attendees know where you're from or other personal details—but only if they're relevant, or if you think they'll somehow warm up the audience.

You want to get to your main point as quickly as possible. The most important part of the pitch is explaining the problem and making people understand the *pain-point*. We recall one guy who got up and explained that he recently bought a present for his girlfriend's birthday. It cost a lot of money and when he presented it to her, he said, "She looked at me like I had kicked a puppy." Suffice it to say, she wasn't thrilled with the item he had chosen. His idea was to create a website that would help men buy gifts for the women in their life, and it was an easy sell after the audience heard that story. Which man in the room *didn't* have that experience? They would all want to check out "Manshopper."

Another entrepreneur wondered aloud about the annoyance of conference calls: Who hasn't had the experience of either forgetting about a conference call or waiting endlessly on one for the other people to join? Whether you're the responsible party or the irresponsible one, the process is irritating. The person presenting a solution for this problem imitated the automated monotone voice that repeatedly requests the six-number code and announces the number of people on the conference call. When he went on to suggest that he could offer a way for your phone to ring when it was time for the call to begin, he had everyone in the room hooked.

When you think about explaining the problem, whether it's to an audience or an investor or your spouse, you should be thinking in terms of problems. Something out there is lacking. People who want to be connected are not being connected. People are unhappy with a service that is already being provided to them, or they can't figure out how to find something better.

It can be something serious, like noting that many individuals are willing to provide shelter to disaster victims while the victims and the larger shelter providers can't find one another. That's what the founder of Sparkrelief explained when he came to Startup Weekend in Denver, Colorado, in October 2010. He had been displaced by wildfires in California and was hoping to help others who had been put in the same position. Today, Sparkrelief "empowers communities and organizations to quickly share accurate information and provide relief during a disaster." The group has been written up in *Time* magazine, received contributions from around the globe, and helped victims of the 2011 earthquakes and tsunami in Japan.

Don't worry, though. You can also pitch a problem that's a little more trivial. Like this one: Don't you love watching TV with your friends? How can you do it when they're not in your living room with you? With an Internet-TV application that offers video chat while you're watching, of course.

Deliver a Solution with One Sentence

So what about the solution? You should be able to summarize it in one sentence. Ignore, for a minute, all of the cool features you'd like to add and focus instead on the core product. How does it solve the problem you've presented? If you've done a good job of explaining the problem, the explanation of the solution should flow naturally.

Now is the time in your pitch to brand your product. Make up a name for your company. Even if it's not the one you will stick with in the end, it's important to leave people with a name to remember. When participants finish their 60 seconds without mentioning a name, we'll usually ask them to come up with one on the spot as they are walking away. Since the audience will be listening to pitch after pitch after pitch, you need to give them something to hang on to and set you apart from the crowd.

Angel investors and venture capitalists may not have 50 or 75 people pitching ideas to them in single a day, but they certainly have a lot over the course of a week—particularly when you count all of the people who find out what they do and want to chew off their ears over drinks or at a birthday party. But your audience, at both Startup Weekend and elsewhere, is not comprised of just investors. It's made of customers as well! Think about how many products and services bombard us with their advertising every day, every hour, and every minute via e-mail, texts, tweets, phone calls, television ads, billboards, and even signs on the sides of buses. You need a name to distinguish your product from the rest.

All of this advice about the substance of your pitch is good to understand. It is necessary, as they say, but not sufficient—because you need enthusiasm, too. Even if you are the last person in line to describe your product—and sometimes, you will be—you have to convey as much passion and energy as though it were the beginning of the day. By attending Startup Weekend, you are trying to get people to give up the next two days of their lives to work with you. You are asking for even more commitment in the real world.

Startup Weekend Company Tag Lines

- 123DressMe: Style with a smile!
- Foodspotting: The best foods and where to find them.
- Giant Thinkwell: Fast, fun, and addicting game play.
- Keepstream: Organize your tweets with curation.
- LaunchRock: Create a viral "Launching Soon" page in minutes.
- Memolane: See, search, and share your life.
- Roqbot: Be the DJ.
- SuperMarmite: It's cooking up in your neighborhood.
- Task Ave.: Remember what you need to do, where you need to do it.

For this reason, you have to be committed to the idea yourself, as well as inspire the commitment of others.

Many Startup Weekend participants tell us that it takes them a few tries to *get the hang of it*; that is, they have to come to a few events before they really master the pitch. But even if you're really not that enthusiastic about your idea, there's no harm in trying it out. Some people we talk to have a list of ideas for startup ventures a mile long and just pick one at random when they arrive on Friday night. But when you're done with your own pitch, you want to watch for other people who have real passion. Those people have that vital first ingredient—*energy*—required to make a successful startup team. While you shouldn't be afraid to get up and offer your idea, you don't want to be too proud to put it on the back burner if you hear something that sounds more promising.

Build a Team

With a firm understanding of action-based networking and the art of the pitch, you can move on to the next phase of starting up a business: building a team. We ask everyone to make sure they tell us exactly whom they need in order to build their product at the end of their pitch. In part, that means assessing your own skills and figuring out what you are lacking. Are you a developer who really needs some de-sign expertise, or a designer lacking any sense of business development? Now is the time to acknowledge where your idea needs some help and expertise.

But maybe you also want to see what other domains are like—in other words, try on another hat. Maybe you're very good at coding but you'd really like to see if you're ready to work on the business end. You'd want to get other developers to join your team so you're not the only one doing that specific task; this will free you up to work on other aspects of the project. It's a good way of building new skills that you might not be able to hone during your day job because the risks are too high. You might find out that you are good at something else; or you might realize you're terrible at it. The crucial thing to keep in mind is that you have nothing to lose. In much the same way that we put our products through multiple iterations, it's important to put ourselves through them. That's what entrepreneurs do.

Sean Kean, a former flight attendant who has been doing computer coding for 20 years, came to his first Startup Weekend looking to expand his horizons a bit. He has now tried the business end of things, and says that Startup Weekend allowed him to figure out the answer to the questions: "Where am I most valuable? Where can I be most effective?" Lately, he spends most of his time talking to investors and customers, and very little time coding. He says his partners are relieved because they prefer to be working on the back end of the project.

Keep in mind that you may not get everyone you want on your team. We try to bring together relatively equal numbers of designers, coders, and businesspeople, but we don't force people to join specific teams. Therefore, some teams have more than their share of one type of worker, and not enough of another. But that's just another challenge to overcome.

What You Need—Talent and Energy

Startup Weekend will help you learn the difference between what you want for your startup and what you need. You may want thousands of dollars, a legal adviser, a research team, and some gourmet food; however, you won't find any of those at Startup Weekend. But you will find what you *need*—talented, energetic people who are willing to adapt themselves to a project (and plenty of energy drinks).

When it comes to finding the right people for your team, the Startup Weekend crowd can be difficult. It is loud and people haven't organized themselves alphabetically or categorically. But in many ways, the chaos that follows the pitches at Startup Weekend mimics the real world. How can you get yourself heard over the din? How can you convince the right people to join your team, even *before* you have funding or customers? You have to worry about winning them over—and not just as part of a big audience listening to your 60-second presentation. You also have to make the case to them one-on-one. It's the difference between auctioning off a date with yourself to any takers in the crowd and finding the person you'd really like to take to dinner and convincing him or her to come along. How do you get to "Great, pick me up at 8"? or, as you hear it at Startup Weekends, "Meet me at the whiteboard with your dry-erase marker and laptop in 20 minutes"?

If you're an entrepreneur trying to assemble a team, you need to convince the talent to join you. Ask them questions about their vision for the project and what they can bring. Find out more about their background, and share more of yours. Give them all the relevant information they need to make a decision.

Have you ever seen a commercial where you had no idea what product or service was being sold?

When preparing a pitch—be it for a startup, a fundraising drive, or to convince your friends to go to Las Vegas with you—always focus on the information the "viewer" most needs in order to understand you.

Then there are those people who, though very passionate about their ideas, have difficulty when it comes to communicating them. Nick Seguin, Manager of Entrepreneurship at the Kauffman Foundation, says that while it helps for an entrepreneur to be driven, the passion is not going to save you if you can't get other people on board. If you're having trouble finding teammates, "you have to be able to extract yourself from the situation and figure out how to either (1) communicate the vision [more clearly] or (2) evolve the vision so you can get people on the same page with you."

As we noted previously, your idea will only be a portion of what attracts people to your company. It will mostly be because of *you*—their understanding of what it will be like to work for and with you. A number of the most successful leaders at Startup Weekend have told us that they never turn down an offer of help, and that a successful leader can find a place for everyone on the team. While this is not always true in the real world, at Startup Weekend people do generally come with useful skills and a willingness to work. That's why most attendees don't turn down too hastily anyone else's offer to join their team.

Richard Grote, a startup veteran from Boulder, Colorado, said that Startup Weekend reminds him of working in his father's service station. "If you're standing around and not doing anything, he'll give you a lot of crap. So you just pick up a broom and start sweeping if you can't think of anything else to do. I think Startup Weekend is one of those places you just want to stay useful and busy."

Nicholas Gavronsky wrote about his experience launching a startup called Animotion at Startup Weekend New York City in the spring of 2011. The idea was to let people create videos on their iPhones that looked like a series of stop-action photographs. He had heard every successful entrepreneur he's met tell him that the team was "absolutely critical." After the event, he wrote the following on his blog: "Every time I hear this, I nod my head and say, 'oh yeah, of course that's important'— without necessarily understanding the team dynamics that you need in order to execute." He didn't know his teammates before they came together, but "from the second we sat down and started working, it was seamless. It was something I hadn't really experienced before, not even in college and the multitude of group projects I had to complete."

Before coming to Startup Weekend, Gavronsky had tried and failed to launch two other startups. "I finally realize [that happened] because the teams [I built] weren't strong enough. [It wasn't] due to a [missing] skill set or domain expertise, but rather to the lack of chemistry and ability to complement each other's strengths and weaknesses. Once you are able to do this—and work seamlessly like we did—it creates a passion and relentless determination to execute perfectly."

Finally, make sure you are absolutely clear about your interests and plans when you are talking to people about joining your team. Do you want to pursue this project in the long term? Is this just something you're trying out on the side? Do you expect to become the CEO of this company with the other team members working for you, or do you hope that you'll all be partners in the startup that comes out of this? There is no right answer to these questions. While we do think that the CEO model doesn't work as well in a three-person operation, of course, the most important thing is being transparent about your motives and your plans. There should be no surprises come Monday morning.

- Do you have a good idea of what sort of people you're looking for?
- Do you have a plan or a tentative timeline?
- Do you know which tasks to allocate to which skill sets?

3

Experiential Education

Step Outside Your Comfort Zone While Working Together as a Team

Now you're ready to get down to the work required in launching a startup. Think of Startup Weekend as a kind of education—what the experts call *experiential education*.

One of our core beliefs at Startup Weekend is that in order for entrepreneurs to learn, they must *do*. Attendees are expected to work with a team at each of our events. They are encouraged to use their creativity to brainstorm, innovate, and problem solve, and use their analytic skills to build solutions, overcome obstacles, and meet real market needs. Regardless of whether a person comes from a tech background or spends her day immersed in business, everybody is asked to tap into all of their talents in order to come up with solutions.

The Startup Weekend Core Team spends a lot of time explaining this theory and proving that experiential education works. Yes, it is often messy, and it is pretty much always unpredictable. But when you force people to dig deep into themselves and their abilities, you're able to draw more out of them than they knew they had to give.

The best analogy to this process is probably learning languages. Sean Kean, the former flight attendant and attendee of multiple Startup Weekends, told us that he spent six years studying Spanish and never used it very much. He says he "can't do anything functional in Spanish." But he spent a year and a half in Japan and is now fluent in Japanese. Coming to Startup Weekend is like "going there"; in other words, it's total immersion in startup culture.

Michael Marasco has set up a program at Northwestern University called Nuvention that is based on the experiential-learning model. He explains his reasoning behind having students actually start up an organization in his class, rather than just looking at case studies of other businesses that have been launched: "We want to help students understand [how] the process [that emerges] from figuring out an idea or a problem really represents the basics of a business—[from the way] you actually build a business around that, to how you pitch it to potential investors." Marasco explains, "Case studies can only bring you so far."

Experiential education is invaluable for early stage entrepreneurs. However, it can also be a way of life for anyone in *any* organization. It may require a bit more effort, but most of the people we encounter find that experiential learning is more enjoyable, too. While there are always failures, the successes feel more real, and more exciting. And that is probably because they *are*.

In addition to preaching the power of experiential education at our events, Startup Weekend also walks the talk and gives employees the daunting but exhilarating task of working via experiential education. One Startup Weekend employee recounts her interview with us: "In the beginning, our connection was quite basic. They knew I was a marketer and I knew that they needed marketing done." But since that time, she has ended up working in just about every area of the company. As she says, "I believed in the vision and the team, and they believed in me. Everything else that has come out of my job since that first interview has been the direct effect of experiential education."

We try to empower anyone who comes to work for Startup Weekend by asking them to create their own job descriptions. We push them to work outside their comfort zones by experimenting with different initiatives, tasks, and goals. It's exactly what we encourage the entrepreneurs at our events to do. You don't have to join a startup or launch a company to see the power of experiential education. As one of our participants claimed, "Not everyone wants to wants to be an entrepreneur; [however], most people want to [improve] themselves . . . and there is no better way to do this than through experiential education."

> Although situations where you are a student rather then an expert can be a bit nerve-wracking, it's also true that you come out of them with new-found confidence in addition to a new skill.
>
> Can you think of a time when you learned a new skill through learning-by-doing?

The Importance of Context, Deadlines, and Instant Feedback

There are some very important components that make up a successful experiential education. The first, which advertisers have learned over the years, is *context*. If you want people to understand that they should buy your cupcake, then you should put a sign outside your cupcake store and maybe even show a picture of someone eating it. It's not that people don't know what to do with a cupcake or where to buy one; it is simply that seeing advertisements in context helps our brains process the message more effectively.

In a similar vein, we can lecture people over and over about what is necessary for starting a successful business from the ground up. However, unless they are actually *going through* the steps that are required to do so, they will not absorb as much information. A number of universities are beginning to realize this, and are adding this kind of education to their business curriculum. Once you realize that you don't need to get a degree before you can start a business, there's no reason *not* to start one while you're working toward your degree!

The second important element of experiential education is *deadlines*. There needs to be an imminent reason to complete the task in front of you. Beth Altringer, who teaches a seminar at Harvard that uses the principles of experiential education, explains how the groups she teaches don't really coalesce around an idea until right before their midterm presentation. "A deadline is [helpful] for a group that has a good idea, because it forces them to think it through more deeply. It forces them out of the brainstorming, conceptual phase." Our deadlines at Startup Weekend may be tighter than most, but we want to move people quickly through these different stages to ensure that they learn from each experience.

What's your attitude toward deadlines?

Just like anything else, the more familiarity you have with them, the less daunting they seem. Break big projects up into smaller pieces and set individual task deadlines. We've found that checking multiple tasks off the To-Do list generates great momentum.

The time limits that Startup Weekend places on participants forces them to narrow their tasks down to the most vital ones. As one participant reported, "Startups thrive only when there are constraints. By locking ourselves into this weekend-long sprint, we were forced to make tough decisions and refine the problem, solution, and market down to their very essential cores."

Eric Koester—a veteran Startup Weekend attendee and now cofounder of Zaarly (a marketplace where people can buy and sell products or services from each other on the spot)—says, "It is critically important to understand how short a time 54 hours really is. Basically, you need to have a minute-by-minute plan of what's going to happen and what it's going to take to get something that you can show-case on Sunday night." He recommends visualizing the presentation and then "working your way backward." If it seems too overwhelming, then you just have to pare back. "Start pulling out the gasket, the fan—all those kinds of things [that allow you to] have an engine that will turn on and [give you something to] show to the audience."

Nicholas Gavronsky, whose team at Startup Weekend New York City created Animotion (now an iPhone app) says that simplicity was the key to their success: "We came up with hundreds of ideas and additional features. Many [people assume that] the more features you add, the better [the end product will be]." But Gavronsky and his team dis-agreed. "Too many features overwhelms users and takes the focus away from what you are trying to do. Ultimately, you need to [concentrate] on the core of the idea, iterate, and launch the most simplistic version." Of course, you can al-ways build it out later on.

The final aspect of experiential learning that we have found to be important is the instant feedback it frequently provides. A formal classroom setting usually requires you to turn in assignments every so often to get feedback from a professor. If you use some of the principles we discuss in the next chapter, you will find that you can get immediate in-put from many different people (i.e., potential customers) about what you've built, or even what you're planning to build. Sorting through that information—and some of it may be contradictory—is a difficult process. However, there is no substitute for learning it firsthand and turning back to apply it to your project.

Nick Seguin, who says that attending Startup Weekends is like a drug for him, has been amazed at what people will teach themselves under pressure. "There's a necessity part of the experience; I can't get anyone else to do it, so I'm going to Google things, look them up, and figure out how to do it myself." Because time's a wasting!

Braindump

So, let's get back to the actual Startup Weekend experience. The first thing we ask participants to do is a *braindump*. Friday is a late night at Startup Weekend. The teams often aren't assembled until after 10 PM; however, people are excited by then and want to start working. The beginning of any startup should involve getting all the ideas on the table. It's the group leader's job to make sure to give others a chance to offer their feedback. It's important to set the tone early for letting everyone have a chance to give input. At the end of Friday night, we find the whiteboards in the room are covered with lists and diagrams. Looking at these is a good way of understanding how ideas truly evolve.

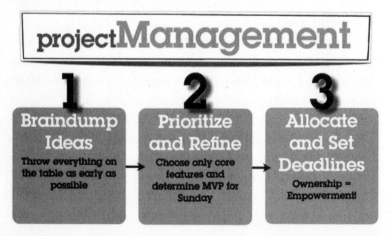

project**Management**

1 **Braindump Ideas**
Throw everything on the table as early as possible

2 **Prioritize and Refine**
Choose only core features and determine MVP for Sunday

3 **Allocate and Set Deadlines**
Ownership = Empowerment!

Limit scope and simplify early!

Sometimes this braindump can result in a complete change of plans. For example, we witnessed one team begin with the idea of creating a mobile application for bars. As you walked around a neighborhood, it would tell you what bars were nearby and what kind of drinks they were offering. Bar owners could send coupons instantly to the app's users to attract them to their establishments.

However, after doing a little digging on Friday night, this team realized that someone had just created this application and released it two weeks before. And they had done it really well. The team tried to think of ways to improve on what was out there, but ultimately decided to go in another direction. They looked at three other possible ideas that various members suggested. One was too technically difficult to accomplish quickly, and another didn't seem as marketable.

Finally, they arrived at their idea for Quotify. This was a site that would allow users to type in funny remarks that their friends made, take a picture of them, and then—after some random interval had passed (four days, four weeks, whatever)—the site would send users back their friend's funny quotation.

The team members determined that it would be possible to design such a site over the course of a weekend, and that there was a market for it. They explained that what would distinguish them was the lack of immediacy. Usually when your friends say funny things, you can tweet them or post about them on Facebook. However, those quotes often get buried in the endless feed of other updates. So wouldn't it be great if these funny moments could come back to you at a later date? They would help to facilitate running jokes among friends.

The idea didn't win that weekend, but the team worked very well together. Because there were only six members, they were stuck in one of the smaller spaces available—a cramped, windowless conference room—for hours on end. They would open the door to get some air and then close it again when they wanted to practice their presentations or discuss strategy. The team's leader was good-natured, and even when they started feeling pressure on Sunday to get everything in order, his self-deprecating humor helped. When it came time to prepare their presentation, they wanted to use a voice recording with sound effects. Two of the team members had a vague sense of how to use the program Garage Band, but they had to work together because neither of them knew it thoroughly. It would be easy to see this team working together again—whatever their next idea might be.

A woman on the team, who had a background in business development, said she had come to one previous Startup Weekend, but her team there was plagued by drama the whole weekend. The team leader apparently got a call from an investor at AOL at some point during the weekend and started badmouthing the other team members. Nothing came of it; needless to say, investors didn't want to hear about the team's internal disputes. And the other team members were pretty angry at the team leader for going behind their backs. These sorts of stories are rare at Startup Weekend, thankfully, and we do everything we can to make sure that people understand the atmosphere of trust is one we have to protect. It is true that some teams just have better chemistry than others; again, it's just like dating. However, if you focus on the task at hand instead of your next move as an individual, success is more likely.

The environment of Startup Weekend—namely, the fact that it *is* a competition—does help to bond a team together more quickly. As one Startup Weekend Baton

Rouge participant told us, "Tension is an understatement during these 54 hours. Reality TV shows could probably be filmed from these events, as the competitors are very intense and focused. Some people might try to tell you that they are there just to learn, but don't be fooled; we are entrepreneurs! Competition is in our nature, along with thirst for recognition."

So You Have a Viable Idea—Now What?

Once you have something that looks like a viable idea, it's time to quickly refine and prioritize. What is the most important aspect of this product? There are at least two schools of thought at Startup Weekend on this question. Some people say the most important thing is to *build something* during the course of the weekend. Indeed, many Startup Weekend participants are builders by nature and by profession. They come because it's fun to build—and to build quickly. They want to test the limits. And they feel like unless you can give customers something to try out, you won't know how to move forward with your business. One of the guys who believed in this very strongly built a system that would complete the conference calling function described in Chapter 2. You simply schedule a call in your Google calendar, and all of the phone numbers on the list would be called and then connected at the appointed time. He demonstrated exactly how it worked for everyone on Sunday night.

The other school of thought is that you need only come out of the weekend with a well-developed idea. Just put up a website offering an idea for a new product or service and ask people if they'd like to buy it. Get people to sign up and tell them you'll let them know when it's ready. Then you'll have some clue about what people want and you won't even have to waste the energy and time and money on building it. This is what business theorists call a proof of concept.

We encourage people to go one step further at Startup Weekend and build what's called a minimum viable product. Rather than just having a website that shows people what the product will do once it's built, go ahead and build a stripped down version of it. As one of the pioneers of this theory, Eric Ries, explained in an interview with Venture Hacks, "The idea of minimum viable product is useful because you can basically say: Our vision is to build a product that solves this core problem for customers . . . we think that . . . early adopters [of] this kind of solution will be the most forgiving. And they will fill in the features that aren't quite there in their minds if we give them the core, tent-pole features that point [in] the direction of where we're trying to go."

Dan Rockwell, who has launched a number of startups and participated in a Startup Weekend in Columbus, Ohio, offers a concise way of thinking about minimum viable products: They should be products with the minimum value, the minimum desired experience, the minimum cash lost, the minimum BS to endure—and the maximum momentum to burn.

Rockwell's company, Big Kitty Labs, produces something called *Protobakes*, which are "functional code examples" of something you want to make at the level of a minimum viable product. He sees these protobakes as a means of facilitating conversation between you and your team, as well as your customers and your investors. To think about a product's growth as a kind of conversation is to understand how quickly and nimbly its development is coming along. As it is when people are talking back and forth to one another, the product model can turn on a dime. This is called *pivoting*.

We talk more about how to get this feedback from early adopters and some of the other methodologies you will see in action at Startup Weekend in the next chapter. For now, suffice it to say that teams at Startup Weekend need to figure out what they can accomplish with the time, resources, and talent they have.

Learning by Doing

Whether or not Startup Weekend participants develop their ideas fully into functioning prototypes by the end of the event, they are always learning by doing. Startup Weekend offers true experiential education. In fact, one graduate of California Polytech told us that this was the aspect of Startup Weekend he most appreciated. As someone who came "from a learn-by-doing environment," he explains that he particularly liked how Startup Weekend is not only showing people how to unlock their entrepreneurial potential, but "letting them try it in a way that shows them that they truly can make their dreams happen." While this individual had attended a number of seminars in school where entrepreneurs had come to *speak* about their experiences, he said it was something else altogether to try out a new business "right then and there."

> Opportunities for experiential education can be found in all areas of life. From cooking classes to flying lessons, learning means rolling up your sleeves and getting to work!

Bo Fishback, cofounder of Zaarly, says he had seen just about every idea out there to encourage the formation of startups in his former role as Vice President of Entrepreneurship at the Kauffman Foundation. Any program that tried to support entrepreneurship inevitably came to Kauffman looking for financial support. He says it is the experiential learning component of Startup Weekend that sets it apart from the rest, even calling Startup Weekend "the single most powerful force for good on planet Earth."

Fishback, who recently left Kauffman to work on a startup that was born at Startup Weekend, explains why our model is distinctive. Though he has an MBA from Harvard, Fishback believes that he learned about a third as much about startups in two years at Harvard as you do in a Startup Weekend. He calls experiential education "the magic ingredient."

Historically speaking, in order to get that experiential education, you had to take a big risk, gamble on a lot of things, and go and work at a startup. You had to quit your job to build a company, or do it in your basement at night and make your spouse mad. Now, there has been a convergence of forces to change that reality.

It's not like Startup Weekend did this singlehandedly. Elements like the availability of technology, the Internet, development tools, and social networking have all contributed to the current environment. What Startup Weekend adds is the practical layer that ties all of that other stuff together.

But there has also been a change in the perspective of young people today, says Northwestern's Michael Marasco. "These are students who live in families where Mom and Dad don't have lifetime employment. They have been restructured, or let go for reasons that were outside their control—and in many cases, it probably had significant [financial and social] impacts on their family." Marasco believes that situation has encouraged his students to "take more control of their lives" by exploring entrepreneurship.

One Startup Weekend participant in Baton Rouge, Louisiana, tells a story of coming to this revelation about entrepreneurship later in life: "I've spent a lifetime working in bureaucracies, not knowing how to break free. But entrepreneurship always tugged at my soul, telling me there is something better to aspire to; [that] there are people who strive for more . . . who are encouraged by their successes and wiser for their failures."

Risk Mitigation

Fishback acknowledges that there is plenty of chaos in the 54 hours of Startup Weekend. But at some point, "You get to piece together what it actually takes to be smart about building a company." Society likes to think of these startup founders as Great Wild West, gun-slinging risk-takers who go out there and hit the right nerve at the right time, and all of a sudden become Bill Gates. There tends to be a certain kind of lore built up around legendary entrepreneurs—how they risked everything on that one brilliant idea.

However, Fishback thinks that those kinds of stories are "total bullshit, actually." Of the thousands of entrepreneurs with whom he has worked, most seem to be "people who are successful and not just lucky—[who] are actually the great *risk mitigators*." Startup Weekend does attempt to be a tool for alleviating risk. It provides entrepreneurs with some visibility, some exposure to schools of business thought, different kinds of human beings—all the elements that essentially let people "try before you buy."

People who become successful entrepreneurs are most often the ones who look into this big cloud of ambiguity—and then, by taking a little step in and looking around, discern whether they can eliminate some of the ambiguity, and then take another step in. This is the process of learning as you go, taking account of the feedback you get from customers, from the market, from the environment—and planning your next move accordingly.

That's why the presentations on Sunday evening often sound different—sometimes entirely dissimilar—from the pitches on Friday night. Some ideas change so completely because participants must undergo the process of discovering what customers want, and what real needs are out there. This is actually all part of that risk mitigation. But the great thing about Startup Weekend is that you can go accomplish this process in 54 hours instead of five years.

The blogosphere and scores of social networking websites have profoundly changed the way we transmit information. Nowadays, you have at your disposal the ability to test ideas, reach distinct communities, and talk to specific customers. One of the reasons the last Internet bubble ended up being a bust is that people were taking risks without gathering, and utilizing, enough of that kind of feedback. Sure, there were a few big successes. But much smarter companies are being built today. It's entirely possible to think to yourself, "Hey, I'd like to try out an idea. Let's see if the market will like it." And you don't have to wait years or months to find out whether your plan will work; it's a matter of days or even hours. We predict that this kind of information gathering will lead to a real entrepreneurship boom.

One startup veteran told us that he was particularly appreciative of the "brutal feedback" he got from other Startup Weekend participants: "[It's] the kind of feedback that makes you reexamine everything that you are doing, [and] that makes you restart and redo everything you've done over and over again."

> Opening yourself and your ideas to criticism can be extremely difficult. Do you have a list of people you can trust who can offer expert critiques? Who can you reach out to for constructive criticism?

The team that built the Internet-TV application decided not to have a live demo of the video chat feature when they introduced their product Sunday night. They reasoned that everyone knows this technology is available. Therefore, they decided to focus instead on getting the application (which displayed what someone's friends were watching) up and running, and then just show people via a slide where the video chat would pop up on the screen.

Allocating Tasks

Once you determine as a team what you can get done in a weekend, you then need to allocate the tasks amongst members. In some cases, it will be obvious who should be doing what. Coders will code. People who specialize in business development will research what else is out there and get customer feedback. Design people will probably be pulled into various different projects. But ultimately, we recommend coming up with a list of discrete tasks and displaying it where everyone can see.

Some teams use the concept of a scrum board in order to show what has been done, what is being done now, and what needs to be done. One advantage of this approach is that everyone on the team knows where things stand. It means that if you want to begin working on a task but feel you can't get started until someone else completes his task, you know to whom you should talk. You keep the workflow going and don't allow it to get bottled up in any one place.

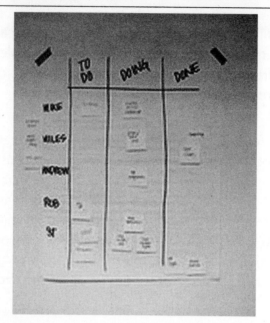

*A basic scrum board shows the status of many tasks that are in a team's pipeline all at once.

Another idea we recommend is an *urgent and important matrix*: a diagram of four squares with one axis labeled *important* and the other labeled *urgent*. Looking at where tasks fall in this matrix makes it immediately obvious what you should be working on *right this minute*.

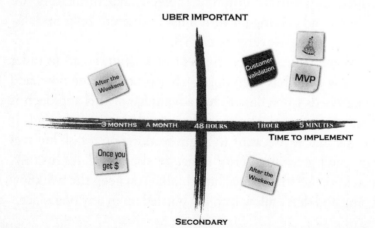

Here Is the Order in Which You Should Complete Tasks:

1. Urgent and important
2. Important but not urgent
3. Urgent but not important
4. Not urgent or important

Once you prioritize as a team, everyone should be clear on what he or she should be doing individually. Giving each person his or her own area in which to work means that everyone will take ownership of their respective tasks, and feel empowered to complete them.

We also recommend that each person only work on one task at a time. The more people are distracted by other priorities, the less effective they will be. Everyone should have a discrete project they are tackling, and it should be in line with the group's overall priorities.

The team leader doesn't have time to be micromanaging everyone; and it's a waste of time for him or her to do so, anyway. If you've put together a group of competent people, let them do their jobs and arrange them in such a way that people don't have to ask permission to go to the next step.

People are always thinking about deadlines at Startup Weekend, and Sunday at 5 PM is always looming. Admittedly, we do try to pack a lot of work into two and a half days. However, this helps to affirm the view we strongly take: that every entrepreneur should always be thinking in terms of deadlines. You want to constantly set short-term goals—something that you can accomplish in a couple of weeks. The further away you make the deadline, the less accountable you will be. So be realistic about the amount of time, but challenge yourself a little, too. After all, we live in a fast-moving business environment. Sitting on an idea for months or a year while you find large chunks of time to work on it will ensure that your competitors will pass you by.

When you're working in the real world, we recommend checking in with your team daily or once every few days. However, people should check in every couple of hours at Startup Weekend. You don't want your team members to waste time going off on the wrong track or to get stuck on a problem that other people may be able to help solve.

Of course, there is always the potential for disagreement on matters that do require the whole group's input. If you've ever been called for jury duty, you know how long it can take for a committee to make decisions. When you assemble a team of smart, informed, and friendly people, you could sit around all day discussing which strategy to take. In fact, we have seen teams spend Friday night and all of Saturday talking about what will work and what won't. Our advice: Don't get sucked into extensive debate. Set a timer for the discussion; talk about an important decision for 20 minutes. If it's not that critical, allow 10 minutes and then take a *Roman Vote*: Everyone gives a thumbs-up or -down. Then, don't look back. Fortunately, moving ahead in startups doesn't always require unanimity the way a jury does. So, see what the majority says—and then move on.

Recognizing Failure

Why is it so important to entrepreneurs to move *fast*? Startup Weekend imposes strict time constraints because there are time constraints in the real world, too. People have day jobs, families, or both. They can't take an infinite amount of time with an idea. You don't want your great idea to be outdated—or accomplished by someone else— by the time you decide to do something about it.

It is not necessarily that speed will equal success; however, moving more quickly *will* let you get to success faster. You need to recognize when you are succeeding and when you are failing. That is, the more ideas you try as an entrepreneur—different products, audiences, monetization strategies, site designs, and so on—the more you will learn. People fail multiple times each weekend, and that's okay.

For example, we once heard a pitch on a Friday night for something called Hoy Hoy, a site that would help people in developing countries use an SMS (text) system and electronic banking to pay each other. In areas where there are few banks and people don't have access to a lot of paper currency (or it's dangerous to carry around too much), this system would give people another option.

By the time we caught up with them on Saturday afternoon, the team's ideas had undergone two more iterations. First, they decided to work instead on the idea of a group savings account. For example, let's say that you and your roommates wanted to save up for a television or a trip. This would be a way to do it. They discussed this idea for a while, trying to determine how the money would be managed. Would one person get to be in control of the money and act as a sort of administrator, or would everyone be in control of their own money? What if someone wasn't meeting a savings goal? Would they be able to default for a month or borrow money against what they had already submitted? Wouldn't too many disputes about money result? The idea seemed to be growing more complicated.

The next version of their plan was for a site to which people were saving for a group trip, contributed equally, and could only take out their own money. But again, the question arose: Who would pay for this service? This continued to plague the group throughout the course of the weekend. On Sunday, one of the mentors who frequently attends Startup Weekend dropped by and started listening to the team, and immediately recognized a successful market strategy. A friend of hers who runs a travel website had often complained to her that he had no way of figuring out people's intentions when they came to his site. Were they daydreaming about a honeymoon in Hawaii with a husband they had yet to meet? Or were they planning a trip to Denver next week and pricing different options?

When the mentor heard about this team's plan, she immediately grasped the potential. A group of people saving for a trip together and actively putting money aside would be the perfect audience for travel websites. Even if some people backed out or some trips didn't happen, at least you would have a good idea of people's intentions. You could figure out where they wanted to go, how many people were traveling, when they planned to leave, what their budget was—all extremely valuable data. In addition to surveying people at Startup Weekend about whether they would use such a site to plan a trip, the team members also called travel company employees to ask if they would be interested in advertising to the site's users, or actually attaching the site to their own product.

Finding out whether there is a market for your product is a vital part of Startup Weekend; it's something we call *idea validation*. This theory of how to start a business has been around for a long time. Decades ago, it was called *bootstrapping*. Now, it's referred to as developing an *agile* or *customer development* model. We talk more about all of these terms in the next chapter—but whatever you call it, the most important thing to understand about this approach is that it is *not* a traditional business plan.

Instead of forming an elaborate strategy of what the entire product will look like, who the consumers will be, and how much money it's projected to make three years down the line, we recommend starting small and working with the information you can get immediately. For example: Who will want this product tomorrow? We always warn people in their Sunday presentations against predicting some ludicrous amount of revenue five years down the line. No hockey-stick growth curves allowed! There are generally no real justifications for their assumptions, and investors are not particularly interested in these projections anyway. They simply want to see the problem, the solution, and how you will ultimately find and satisfy your customers with your product.

Can you explain the most basic feature of your idea?

Remember, basic does not necessarily mean simplistic. Basic ideas are fundamentally important and provide the foundation off of which every fancy feature is built.

A good place to start is with your immediate circle of friends. Throughout the event, you'll see team members wandering around, asking other people whether they can offer opinions on a product. The aforementioned group that was interested in helping men shop for women found a few females and asked them what kind of gifts they like. They then asked men what kind of help they needed when shopping for the women in their lives.

It's so easy these days to send out a survey to a larger group as well. It's as simple as finding a few relevant questions to ask and posting them on your Facebook page. The

Internet-TV application team asked people if they would like to watch TV with their friends in different locations. Some groups announce their product online for potential users to test, or to encourage people to sign up for it when it becomes ready for testing. It's important to get the market's pulse as quickly as possible.

The Three Main Criteria

By Sunday morning, energy levels start to flag. Tension builds on some teams as members have to make tough decisions about how to guarantee that they have a viable presentation to give by 5 PM. If there is ever a time for the team leader to assert him- or herself, this is it. Boulder Startup Weekend participant Dave Angulo says that he wouldn't compare the team leader role to that of CEO so much as one of "project manager." He says the important part is "organizing people, understanding where the roadblocks are, making sure you can clear those roadblocks so everyone can keep moving."

It is actually surprising how seldom we see teams argue over who should be the team leader. Usually, one team per weekend might have a couple of alpha entrepreneurs who both want to take charge, and we occasionally have to intervene. But for the most part, everyone there simply wants to work hard. A lot of them come from environments where they have to deal with a lot of bureaucracy and so they don't relish the idea of organizing other people so much as generating a real product.

Still, it is possible to tell on Sunday night the teams who worked well together—which leaders were overbearing and micromanaging, and which ones let things spin a little out of control. Over the course of doing hundreds of these events, we have tried to focus less on how shiny the pitch decks are on Sunday night, and instead concentrate on what people have made and how they've worked as a team. As Dan Rockwell of Big Kitty Labs told us, "Startup Weekend is focused on action. They care less about the bar chart with thousands of potential dollars and more on other questions like—did you get along with your team?" If you can't figure out how to work well within a team, you could have an idea as great as the next Groupon, and it will crash and burn because you can't get over your ego.

At each Startup Weekend, we try to bring together at least three judges who are experienced in the field of entrepreneurship—either successful startup founders or investors. We ask them to judge the Sunday presentations using three main criteria:

1. **Customer Validation:** Did you interview potential or target customers? Did you integrate that feedback into

your products? Have you built a base of fans and would-be customers?

2. **Business Model:** Did you differentiate yourself from your competitors? Did you define your customer acquisition and rollout strategies? Did you clearly and realistically articulate your revenue model?

3. **Execution:** Did you develop a functional prototype? Did you execute it well as a team?

We discuss the first one further in the next chapter on customer development and lean/agile strategies for launching a startup. We do expect teams to show evidence that they have gotten some information from potential customers about what they want.

We should say with regard to criterion 2 that you don't need to go through every other company out there with a similar mission and explain the difference. There may be a number of them. Sometimes judges or members of the audience will ask questions to make sure that you are aware that some of your major competitors do exist. At that point, you can show that you know the market. You have only five minutes during the presentation. (At some Startup Weekends, presentations are even shorter because of the number of teams presenting.) So, you want to spend as much time as possible focusing on your own product.

As we mentioned before, the execution will depend very much on the product. We like participants to have a functioning prototype; however, we realize that this isn't possible in all circumstances. But we do want to come as close as possible to the actual experience users will have with your product. Screenshots of your web page will help, of course. But we still want you to walk us through the *experience* in your presentation.

Even though judges are trying to decide whether you worked well as a team, they do not want to see every one of your team members giving the presentation. Having seven people pass the microphone back and forth wastes time, and looks a lot like a first-grade play. So choose the one or two people with the best stage presence to talk to the audience and the judges. Of course, you want to be sure that they thank the rest of the team in their presentation. (Some people even include a slide in their pitch deck with pictures of their team or at least everyone's name.) When the judges pose questions that the presenter can't answer, they should see if someone else on the team can help.

Now that you know the judging criteria, consider what questions you should be answering with your presentation. The following are some questions that Dan at Big Kitty Labs asks about all of his team's prototypes, which are vital questions for Startup Weekend, too:

- What is it?
- Why do I need it?
- What does it do?
- Who uses it?
- How does it make money?
- How does it provide value?
- Who'd write a story about it?
- How does it work?
- What does it rely on?
- What's it like (experience-wise)?
- Where do the data come from?
- What are the barriers, black boxes, and questions you have no idea how to answer yet?

While our judges always like smooth answers to their questions, try to be honest if you don't know something. It is hard to really get a handle on all of these questions in one weekend. Demonstrate at least that you as a team have the ability and inclination to find out. We want you to accomplish as much as you can in a weekend (or any amount of time), but remember that Sunday night doesn't have to be the end of the project. Rather, those 54 hours can be the beginning of a much bigger experience.

4

The Startup Business Model
Adapt, Stay Lean, and Reiterate

SINCE THE BEGINNING of time, people have started businesses. Some caveman somewhere invented the wheel, and then some other caveman thought, "Hey, that's worth something. Bet I can get some berries or a nice tender piece of woolly mammoth in exchange for it." This went on for thousands of years, even though it wasn't until 1910 that Harvard offered the first MBA degree. But that doesn't mean the MBA didn't add anything. The master's of business administration was the beginning of the formation of a body of knowledge about exactly what it sounds like: how to administer businesses.

People began to formally study a variety of subjects, including marketing, hiring, and finance. They started to look at different tools and models for organizing businesses more effectively. They asked questions like: Who should manage these companies? How much input should employees have? How much inventory should they keep? How do they keep their old customers happy while gaining new customers? How can they adapt to changes in the market?

These were and still are profoundly important questions. However, they are also questions that the MBA curriculum historically addressed for businesses that already existed. They didn't have to be huge corporations, but they had to be somewhat established. Until 30 or 40 years ago, there wasn't really a formula or even much in the way of practical advice for people starting up new businesses. There weren't many books on the subject. And these lessons certainly weren't provided in any kind of classroom setting.

Successful entrepreneurs were considered to be either geniuses or very lucky—people who happen to strike on the right idea at the right time. They didn't have a particular degree or any kind of formal training. They were renegades who saw into the future, knew where the market was headed, realized something about technology or communication or politics, and they pounced. And they probably had to have a little change in their pockets, too— because until recently, very few people found investing in someone else's entrepreneurial ventures to be a particularly good use of their money.

However, the second half of the twentieth century brought the emergence of what we now know as Silicon Valley. It became a home to all sorts of electronics engineering, from radio to television, then on to computers, and now to every kind of high-tech business imaginable. The area also became a sort of laboratory for startup businesses. Because the technology that people were developing there was often brand new, and because so many young people were trying to get their start in the area (many coming out of nearby Stanford University), the region became a center for entrepreneurial activity. And the people who came there didn't necessarily have MBAs or training in larger companies, for that matter. Many were blank slates when it came to an understanding of traditional business practices.

Steven Blank was one such individual who came to Silicon Valley in the late 1970s in the middle of one of the area's booms, during a kind of renaissance for startups. Looking back, he says, "It wasn't that people weren't doing startups when they invented the wheel. It's the combination of technology, entrepreneurship, and risk capital [that become] the 'modern era of entrepreneurship.'"

Blank went on to work for and launch eight different technology companies, including one called Epiphany that developed software to manage customer relationships; two semiconductor companies; a supercomputer firm; a military intelligence systems supplier; and a video game company. Looking back on his career, he says his "total score" was "two large craters, one dot-com-bubble home run, and several base hits."

What really determined the ultimate success or failure of these enterprises? It wasn't until after Blank had left most of this behind that he began to think about the patterns that startups and their leaders seemed to follow. Maybe it wasn't all dumb luck that allowed entrepreneurs to succeed. And maybe the successful ones weren't all geniuses.

But why did success for entrepreneurs seem so completely unpredictable? The reason, Blank says, is that everyone was using the business school model. "Everybody made a fatally bad assumption: that startups were simply smaller versions of large companies." However, according to Blank, "Once you make that assumption, all other bad stuff follows." That means the individuals who launch them manage their startups like miniature models of large companies. But the difference, according to Blank, is really profound: "Large companies execute known business models; startups search for business models."

> ■ Are you having trouble getting started with your idea?
> ■ Is your action plan appropriate given your skills, resources, and constraints?
>
> While it can certainly be motivating to daydream about huge profits, be sure to stay grounded in the reality of your current situation.

What does that mean? In short, Blank says, "When you execute, you have [tactics]. You have processes. You have business plans. You hire people to execute, and any failure is a failure of competence. But when we're searching, there is no plan; in fact . . . failures are part of the process." People are particularly uncomfortable with that part about failure. How do you explain that to employees? How do you explain that to your customers? How do you tell them you are looking for a business model? It's not a phrase that inspires confidence.

Having witnessed his own and other startup problems for years, Blank says, "The same issues arose time and again: big company management styles versus entrepreneurs wanting to shoot from the hip; founders versus professional managers; engineering versus marketing; marketing versus sales; missed schedule issues; sales missing the plan, running out of money, [or having to] raise new money." He says he "began to gain an appreciation of how world-class venture capitalists develop pattern recognition for these common types of problems. 'Oh yes, company X, they're having problem 343. Here are the six likely ways that it will resolve, with these probabilities.' "

Well, maybe it's not *that* exact. Blank talked to a few of his friends in the venture capital business who acknowledged that they had noticed these problems over the years. They had developed a pretty good sense of which firms were going to succeed and which would fail based on these patterns. "But why didn't you tell us?" Blank asked halfjoking. "That's not our job," they laughed. And it's true, Blank says now; venture capital firms aren't in the habit of teaching entrepreneurs how to do their jobs. But still, he thought, *someone* should. Blank was one of the pioneers of this new curriculum, and we'll get to the important ideas he developed in a moment.

We want our Startup Weekend participants to understand the patterns present in successful startups. We want them to realize that success is not entirely based on luck and that you don't have to be prescient or a genius in order to make a go of entrepreneurship. In this chapter, we'd like to explain something about those patterns and talk about some of the methodologies that have been created in order to make sure that today's entrepreneurs can avoid some of the pitfalls of their entrepreneurial forefathers.

We don't want you to see entrepreneurship as something you try once, and then decide is too much of a risk. We also want to remove some of the risk for you, and part of doing that is offering participants some sense of the most effective entrepreneurship techniques. There are plenty of books, articles, and blogs written about the ideas we talk about in this chapter. And we have included a list of references for further reading at the end of the book. But if you're at a Startup Weekend or you're trying to start a business for the first time—and quickly—this chapter gives you a primer on these ideas. If you're already familiar with these methodologies, then Startup Weekend will be a great opportunity for you to try some of them out and see which ones work for you.

The Startup Weekend team strongly believes that businesses flourish or die because of their business *model*—their business plan. Traditional business settings emphasize revenue generation and cash flows. Cutting-edge business trends, however—like those championed by Steve Blank and some of the other thought leaders mentioned in this chapter—urge founders to concentrate on the quality of their ideas and products; and they encourage them to do this, not through the lens of profitability, but by focusing on the overall vision, framework, and team. That's why we discourage people from presenting some ridiculous growth curve for their revenue during their final presentations. We're much more interested in the team, the overall vision, and who has bought into the idea.

The Customer Development Revolution

Steve Blank developed his theory of *customer development* in response to the patterns he saw in startup successes and failures. He began to explain the keys to this idea in his classes at Berkeley and Stanford. The first and most important: Leave the building. Talk to customers. Don't go too far down any road, and don't spend too much time developing any product until you *know what the customers want*.

Blank says that one of the major mistakes startup enterprises make is confusing the founder's vision and passion (which he says is "essentially a faith-based enterprise on Day One") with actual, concrete facts. People who have agreed to work on a startup believe that the founder somehow implicitly understands the customer's problems and needs. They have signed on to do the work because they have a great deal of faith in the business's underlying concept. As we've discussed before, the team and team leader are the elements who should make people want to join—not the idea. Remember: Ideas are a dime a dozen. No founder, no matter how smart, can read customers' minds. And if people confuse their confidence in the founder with their confidence in the idea, then they make the next fatal error. They simply take the founder's vision at face value and conclude, as Blank puts it: "Now I should simply start building the product as per my vision, and when I'm done, I'm going to release it, ship it, and money will just start rolling in."

> Are you a visionary or a worker bee? A good leader has to be both—and inspire others to be both as well.

Customer development essentially states that this is not going to work unless you are randomly lucky or are somehow *the* expert in a particular domain. And the probability that you actually, truly *know* customers' problems and needs on the first day of work is extremely low. So, Blank says, "Why don't we establish a process that eliminates waste and makes learning and discovery an integral part of what you do from its very early stages?"

In Chapter 3, we discussed some suggestions for gauging what people want out of a product. At Startup Weekend, people do quick electronic surveys or walk around the room; however, we also encourage them to literally *leave the building.* It is easy at Startup Weekend or in any startup environment to get so attached to your desk that you never get any fresh input, and the feedback that you get from friends and family will naturally be skewed. (Even if your mother is often critical, she's mostly on your side, right?) So don't just depend on the opinions of those in your immediate circle. Go interview people you don't know and find out what they want. Go to a coffee shop or a nail salon—someplace where people have a little time on their hands. Or stand on the street corner. Eventually, someone will stop to talk.

Most of us are totally afraid of cold-calling someone or starting a conversation with a perfect stranger. We think business has moved beyond that; door-to-door salesmen are a relic of the past, right? But in order to find out what customers want, there is much to be said for talking to people who don't know you from a hole in the wall. Interestingly enough, sometimes strangers are too nice. They don't want to tell you to your face that your idea is terrible. One way around this is to suggest that the idea is someone else's. "My colleague George has an interesting idea for a . . . ."

Once you find people who are willing to talk to you, the trick is asking the right questions. Startup Weekend attendee Nick Martin started a company called Plane.ly, a website that allows you to meet people with similar interests while you're flying. At one point he remembers talking to business owners about their needs. He laid out for them the top three problems he thought that businesses had and then asked them to put them in order. In retrospect, he thinks he was "leading the witness" a little. Why not offer more choices, and then ask your potential customers to add to the list of problems? Customer development conversations are not supposed to be interrogations; they're supposed to be dialogues. The more open-ended you can make your questions, the more useful the information you will get. It's the difference, as every parent knows, between asking a kid, "Did you have fun at school today?" and "What did you do at recess?"

Nathan Bashaw, the founder of Thoughtback.com and a guest speaker at a Startup Weekend in Lansing, Michigan, wrote this advice regarding interviews on his blog. It's worth a read:

Have you ever noticed how the best conversations tend to wander away from the original talking point, and head towards interesting, uncharted territory? When you're talking to potential customers, do everything you can to let these types of engaging discussions emerge. Don't stop them when they're leaning forward in their seat with their eyes wide, adrenaline surging, paying rapt attention to the conversation. I used to take a rigid, formal approach to customer development interviews until I realized that I never got many good ideas or feedback from those conversations. My scripted questions made people uneasy, and they weren't willing to open up with what they *really* think. Now, I don't think of these interviews as anything more than an opportunity to build a relationship and learn from an interesting person. I ask about their story, how they got started doing what they do, what they've been reading lately, where they want to be in five years. This gives me a holistic understanding that no survey will ever be able to replicate, because it takes a genuine human connection for people to feel comfortable opening up.

> Make the most out of potential customers' feedback. Ask questions that can't be answered with a simple "yes" or "no."
>
> Instead of asking someone, "Do you like benefit/ feature X?", ask them, "What about benefit/ feature X most appeals to you? Why?"

The reason to get out there and talk to people you don't know at an early stage is to confirm that there is an actual *need* for the product you want to create. This is called idea validation. While it's probably not possible at Startup Weekend to put the whole project on hold while you validate ideas, it would be useful if someone on the team at least attempted it. (Remember, you're already starting with some idea validation if other people have decided to join your team. *Someone* thinks it's a good idea.)

The goal of idea validation is not selling people on a product; it is to explore the field in order to gain knowledge, not money. Don't be offended by people who don't like your idea. Consider it knowledge gained. Now, you know the direction in which you should *not* take your product. You can be grateful that you've invested nothing but some time and energy in the project at this stage. You haven't created anything yet. And getting feedback now is usually easier for people. Think about it this way:

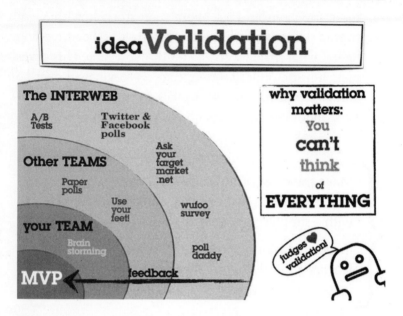

If you threw on a pair of pants and a shirt this morning and barely combed your hair, you would probably shrug it off if someone later made a snide remark about your appearance. (I didn't put much effort in making myself look presentable, so it's not surprising.) But if you went out, got a new haircut, a nice outfit, put on some makeup, and then someone didn't like your appearance, you'd be more upset. (I spent all this time and money and they still don't like the way I look.) While gaining this knowledge will not immediately lead to huge streams of revenue, it is vital to your company's success down the line.

Once you have created your minimum viable product, you can revisit these methods of getting feedback from potential customers to see if they like your product. Remember the basics: Ask people you don't know, and pose open-ended questions about the product. Don't be offended by the results. Just go back and see if you can incorporate the feedback you've gotten into the next version of the product. Try to formulate specific hypotheses about your product. To whom will it appeal? How many visitors do you expect to get at your website? It is important to be specific in order to see how well you are gauging your market.

Remember that old rule about the customer always being right? Well, there's a lot to it. Restaurant owners and people in the service industry are reminded of this concept on a daily basis. It doesn't matter if the guy said he wanted the coffee black and you gave it to him that way. Now he says he wants it with sugar. Don't argue with him; just give him the sugar. And smile. Or he won't come back tomorrow and he'll tell his friends not to as well. However, when you start making things that you're selling to customers who are not right in front of you, the *customer is always right* maxim often gets lost somewhere along the way. Since so many of the people who launched startups came from an engineering background, they were completely removed from the customer experience. The ideas behind customer development represent a revelation for many of them.

A lot of business books out there (for entrepreneurs and anyone else) emphasize *persistence*. The notion is that you should just keep trying your product, and talk about it in different ways. Keep working in your basement and eventually all that hard work will pay off. The bottom line, however, is that it may not. And if you talk to your customers early and often, you will find that out sooner rather than and later and free yourself to move on to an idea that will actually work.

Getting Lean, Staying Agile, Preparing to Pivot

As foundational as Steve Blank was to what has been an entrepreneurial revolution, he says that his theory of customer development is really only one piece of the new curriculum for entrepreneurs. Just as startups have to think about both their business models and marketing plans differently, they also have to think about how the organization operates and how to hire differently. In the years since Blank published his class notes in the form of a book called *Four Steps to the Epiphany*, others have begun to explore and explain these other pieces of the entrepreneur puzzle.

Sometimes they have developed theories and models from scratch. But other times, they have repurposed business theories from large, well-established companies. Toyota, for instance, had begun in the 1950s to use something called *lean* manufacturing to make cars more efficiently. The idea behind it was simply to create less waste. Companies that operate under the lean manufacturing approach try both to reduce waste and increase flow.

When you imagine an assembly line, you usually envision the processing of a large number of things. But lean manufacturing processes a very small amount of items at one time. Everything that is waiting to be produced is inventory, and you want the lowest inventory possible. For instance, it might take someone a short time to make a car door, and a long time to install it. Jeremy Lightsmith, a startup veteran who does consulting on lean strategies for large companies, explains it in the following way: "If you produce, produce, produce, and the thing that takes forever is attaching the door, and then you have all these doors that now you have to store, and if there's an error on the second door now you've made a hundred doors and they all have the same error."

This idea may be even more important to small new businesses than large well-established ones. The small businesses don't have the extra manpower or the extra capital, so keeping inventory to a minimum is vital—and not just on the production line either. This is critical when developing a product as well. That's why entrepreneurs need to create only a minimum viable product and then test it with potential customers immediately. You don't want to create a whole lot of something unless you know customers are going to be happy with it. This approach allows you to take smaller risks.

Software developers became particularly attuned to this problem in the 1990s, and began to work on a methodology that is now called *agile* development. Agile developers use a series of stories in order to make their products. Each of these stories then prompts another iteration of the product. For instance, let's say that you are using a website and want to log out so that the person who uses the computer after you doesn't get a hold of your credit card information. This requires a particular kind of functionality of the website. Solving that problem is a discrete task that can be done in a particular amount of time by a particular individual or group of individuals; it's a story. The time set aside to accomplish that task can be called a *sprint*. In this way, we can think of launching a new business as a series of sprints.

Over time, *agile* has become a type of shorthand for a certain method of project management. In the software realm, which is where people mostly use the term now, agile has come to include the ways in which people write codes and do their designs. The emphasis is on keeping these simple, so everyone on the team can understand them, and so they can be changed down the line without throwing everything off.

There are a variety of tools now available for entrepreneurs to use agile methods in their work. One of them is called *scrum*, which comes from the term for a huddle in the sport of rugby. New entrepreneurs and participants at Startup Weekend don't have to grasp all of the concepts behind the theory of scrum; however, we try to help Startup Weekend attendees pick out some tools they might find helpful during the course of the 54 hours they are with us.

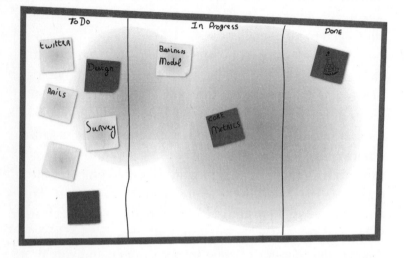

Plane.ly founder Nick Martin had previous experience working with a different project management model called the *waterfall method*. This occurs when you specify a whole bunch of functionality about what a website should do up front. Basically, you put as much in it as possible; then, that specification gets passed from the people who designed it to the people who are going to build it. Those people then build it for a certain amount of time until it's finished. Then there's another team that normally takes over the testing of it. Once it's been tested, and it's signed off, then it goes into production and gets released.

Martin says he became frustrated with this model quickly, and explains, "The problem with the waterfall methodology is that while a specification is being developed and tested, the designers usually get some great new ideas that they want to throw into the mix." So, you either tell the designers they can't integrate those new ideas because it's too late; or, they incorporate the ideas, and then the rest of the team isn't ready for that. Those new ideas get passed through the development and testing phases. And then the different teams will go back and forth. Martin says, "Unless you're very disciplined, you end up with a situation where nothing ever gets released."

Nick remembers one particularly difficult entrepreneur he encountered while working for a startup in Australia. "We had an amazingly inspirational product manager who was kind of responsible for the product design and all the features that [we incorporated]. His brain never turned off, and he was always getting new ideas." While this sounds like a good thing in principle, Nick recalls, "I was the test manager at that stage, so I'd be testing about a specification he had written, but then he'd be writing another one by the time any development ever got to me."

Using other project management techniques can help a team avoid this kind of frustration. The *scrum board*, which we talked about a bit in the last chapter, is one tool we find effective in avoiding this kind of back and forth and internal argument. It's a way of organizing work by type and by stage in the process. It might, for instance, be a marketing task that goes from "needs to be done" to "in progress" to "done." It's a way of visualizing where everyone is in the process. It means that you need only look up for a moment to see where your colleagues are and what they are working on at that moment. In other words, you don't need to keep interrupting to ask.

When these *sprints* are done, a product can be released. The most important mantra behind these methodologies is *release early, release often*. Don't sit on your ideas or your products for too long. Let customers have a look at them, give you feedback, and then change the product to adapt to their needs.

Startup Weekend also demonstrates very easily the utility of some of these tools. If you volunteer to do a particular task for your team, you have to get it done. Everyone knows exactly the tasks for which they are responsible. Jim Benson, who does lean consulting for large companies like Comcast, explains what he likes about Startup Weekend: "You come into a very respectful egalitarian system. You assume that when your teammates sit down at a table and they say, 'I can do this,' that they can do this. And the rate at which you check each other's work is so rapid that you immediately know whether or not someone can deliver on what they say."

Benson says, "People have to be [entirely] honest about what their capabilities actually are, because there's no time to bury it." For example, he says, "If you say, 'Right now I will cook you a chicken,' and then you don't know how to cook a chicken, people are going to figure out pretty quickly when you take the raw chicken and put it in the microwave."

Communication Is Key

The initial brainstorming that is required to produce a scrum board, or any similar kind of chart, also encourages the entire team to make sure their ideas are heard. Usually, one or two people tend to dominate the conversation in large groups that are under time pressure. These individuals may be smart or simply like the sound of their own voices; however, they tend to intimidate their fellow team members and cause others to be reluctant to participate. We're pretty confident that just about everyone who comes to Startup Weekend has something to contribute to the team. So it's important to hear everyone out, particularly at the beginning of the process.

Jeremy Lightsmith says that some of the biggest problems he sees in startups are those that involve communication. In short, someone is not being heard, or there is duplication on a project. One part of the team hasn't passed on some vital piece of information to another.

One startup veteran told us that he will lead the team if it's his idea that's being discussed, but only in a particular way: "The way I work these days is to run workshops with these big pieces of brown paper on the wall. [I then give] everyone a pack of Post-it notes." The group leader sets up the problem, but then asks everyone in the group how they are going to solve it. He says, "It's not going to be my idea; it's going to be [everyone]'s ideas. I'll [ultimately] be accountable for the results, but it's going to be coming from [others as well]."

This approach has other benefits, too; first, it sets the tone for the way in which the group will work. Anyone can feel comfortable to share her ideas through the course of the weekend. Also, people sometimes just have these ideas in the back of their heads. Even if the team doesn't have time to accomplish every idea over the weekend, just getting them out there will allow people to put them aside and possibly come back to them later.

The techniques we encourage people to employ at Startup Weekend can also make them more effective leaders. In a traditional method of project management, everything is planned out ahead of time, and any changes along the way seem to come from the top. However, conducting extensive customer development and then releasing only the minimum viable product allows startup founders to eliminate some of the frustration that their colleagues will feel in the process. There will be more input from the whole team at the beginning of the process. Then, any changes that occur will be based on new evidence that is gathered—not some lightning bolt of inspiration that just happened to strike the leader while everyone else was doing their jobs. The seemingly arbitrary way in which some team leaders change their minds can lead to incredible frustration on the part of their colleagues.

Can you think of other aspects of your life where obtaining group buy-in is necessary?

When trying to gain a group consensus, practice soliciting feedback while keeping control of the debate and ultimately deciding on an action plan.

One Startup veteran illustrates this point by discussing the difference between Captain Kirk of *Star Trek* and Jean-Luc Picard of *Star Trek: The Next Generation*. He says,

> Kirk was kind of the swashbuckling hero who if there was a plan to go down to kick some alien butt, he would be the one leading the team right from the front, and he'd be first one saying, 'Beam me down, Scotty.' Picard, on the other hand, would always stay back at the ship and allow his guys to go come up with the ideas and have all the glory. He'd just sit back in the chair, ask for ideas, and then pick the best one.

In other words, the best leaders are the ones who generate capability and capacity in their staff.

Combining the pace of Startup Weekend with one of the agile methods of dividing up tasks makes everything more transparent. And that can have excellent benefits for startups.

Stick with the Basics

Nick Martin had actually done a lot of reading about lean and agile approaches to business before coming to Startup Weekend. He says: "I was eager to test it out and get involved. The whole concept of basically winning customers who are willing to pay for your product before you get to the point where you even start developing that product [made complete sense]. It's an incredibly attractive idea for anyone who's running a business."

Lean or agile methodologies instruct founders to invest in staying small, streamlining operations, incorporating customer feedback, and pivoting often. The idea is to listen to your customers, adapt quickly, and remain true to your core competencies. While many lean/agile theories are ideal for young companies that are still in the flexible and somewhat ambiguous market penetration or the early growth stages, it makes sense to introduce them at events like Startup Weekend.

In a sense, Startup Weekend teams and ideas are pre-lean/agile. Ideas were pitched (or dreamed up) mere hours ago, and team members were complete strangers when they arrived at the event. It may be a bit premature to expect adherence to Lean practices when you're still trying to explain what your product or service *is*. But lean/agile methodologies still have a lot to offer hours-old ventures. The principles of streamlining operations, organizing projects by task lifecycle rather than competencies, incorporating customer feedback, and pivoting early and often are extremely relevant.

At Startup Weekend, we want people to envision the development of startups as a loop. Come up with an idea, ask people about it, release a minimum viable product, ask people to test it, revise the product, ask them to test it again.

This refining process allows you to correct missteps along the way quickly. If Startup Weekend participants start to use these processes early, then they will learn to integrate them into all of their entrepreneurial ventures.

Interestingly, one of the areas in which people pivot most often is that of monetization. While the question of where your money will come from is the key to the whole enterprise in a traditional business plan, there has to be a different mentality in startups. For example, while individuals might not be willing to pay for a website that allows you to save for trips as a group, travel companies will be interested in reaching those groups. Maybe you have a great search engine but it is not the people using Google who are paying for it; it's the companies that want their ads to come up with the search.

Nick Martin wasn't sure that individuals would be willing to pay for a service that allowed them to meet other people in airports. Although he has had a website up for several months now, his team is still working on the question of who is going to pay for their service. Recently, Martin has started considering the fact that multinational corporations might be his key customers. One of his users asked him about this possibility. He says, "I called them up and went through a customer interview with them to understand what it was that their problems were. Now I'm repeating that process with as many multinationals as I can find."

Nick has been using these lean/agile ideas since he launched his company. It is hard to start using these ideas when you are in the middle of launching a business, particularly one that has already received some funding. Investors expect a product with particular features at a particular time, in addition to some returns. If you scrap the whole plan and decide to go back to the customers in the middle of the process, your stakeholders may get upset.

This is precisely why Startup Weekend is the perfect venue to test some of this out. Is your team divided over a possible feature? Are you clueless as to what the graphic designer sitting next to you is doing and how it relates to your task? Do you feel overwhelmed by the sheer number of things that have to be accomplished? In all of these situations—situations that every Startup Weekend team faces at least once during the weekend—lean/agile methodologies can help with decision-making, product/service development, and task management. Adopting these tools and methodologies does not increase output during the Startup Weekend 54-hour frenzy of activity; however, it does improve the quality of the output. And that can mean a world of difference to a judging panel trying to determine the future viability of your startup.

> You can adapt lean/agile tools to everyday life, too. Next time you're working on a term paper or organizing the costumes for your 12-year-old's class play, create a scrum board in order to visualize the project's progress and keep on top of each task.

We put a lot of emphasis on the time limits of Startup Weekend; they are obviously a salient feature. However, it can be helpful to take some time to organize your team rather than diving right into the project. It may seem like you're wasting precious minutes when you do this, but it can really help in the long run (i.e., the next 24 hours) when the pressure is on. You can put the process in place while things are relatively calm, and then rely on it to carry you through when things start to get crazy.

The Missing Pieces of the Entrepreneur's Curriculum

It is not only the way startups come up with a product that is different from big well-established companies. It is also the presence of risk capital. The money that startups need is not some big or traditional bank loan (and they probably couldn't get one anyway.) As Steve Blank explains, "If you went into a bank and said, 'Listen, I got this portfolio I want to invest in, and 90 percent of the enterprises in it will fail,' they'd laugh you out of the room. This is a financial asset class that's actually based on taking risks." The folks who provide money to startups are rare in that they still consider funding these startups to be a hugely profitable enterprise, despite the small percentage of ultimately successful businesses.

It is also the way, for instance, that they are financed. If you come from a well-established, business-world background, the idea that you would invest in ventures with such a high failure rate would have been considered absurd. But angel investors and venture capitalists have pioneered new ways of thinking about these investments. They try to offer small amounts of seed money to spread the risk around, and expect higher returns on the ventures that succeed. Startup Weekend tries to bring in mentors from the world of startup financing to help entrepreneurs understand the way financing works in this segment of the business world.

There are other pieces of this entrepreneurial curriculum that have yet to be written. One important matter is the question of how to hire the right people for a startup. Startups don't have the money in most cases to hire some HR expert. And for the most part, that's not what they need. Looking for cofounders, or the startup's core team, is a vital part of the process—one that occurs even before customer development.

Happening upon the right cofounder is a critical part of Startup Weekend. We talked a little about how to go about this in the chapter on action-based networking. But what are the skills you are looking for? It may sound obvious, but startups need people who are flexible. There isn't money to fund a lot of the frills people take for granted at big companies, and there aren't any assistants to help out. People do their own photocopying and shipping and faxing and scanning at Mail Boxes Etc. They don't ask someone else to do it for them.

There will inevitably be days where people will be forced out of their comfort zones. There's going to be that big meeting where one person was expected to do the pitch but got sick and someone else had to fill in. There will be a project that needs to get done quickly and so the design people are pulled off of what they're doing to help the marketing person. You need people who will work on an idea as if their lives depended on it but then turn on a dime when the customers say they need something different, and work on the new idea with the same kind of intensity. You need people who respect each other and work well together in small spaces under tight deadlines without a lot of money. Maybe there's not going to be a textbook that explains how to find these people, but this is exactly where Startup Weekend can help fill in the missing pieces of the entrepreneur's curriculum.

Mapping the Startup Ecosystem and Subversive Reconstruction

WHAT DOES IT take to become an entrepreneur? That's a question a lot of people have been asking themselves. Whether you have a steady job, you're retired, or you're just out of school; whether you've been laid off during this Great Recession or you're thinking of marching out of your cubicle on your own tomorrow—how do you figure out if you have what it takes to launch your own startup? Our advice: Don't wait for lightning to strike. Most people don't become successful entrepreneurs because they have a sudden revelation about a brilliant idea for a business model. And nobody is born an entrepreneur, either. Just because you haven't started your own business before doesn't mean you can't do it as early as tomorrow.

Becoming an entrepreneur is a process. It doesn't require total commitment on the first day, and—as with any professional opportunity—prudence is just as important a factor as boldness. Before you hand in your resignation or tell off your boss, before you even clear out your garage to start tinkering and tell all your friends what your plans are, begin by dipping your toe in the water.

A lot of the people who come to Startup Weekend are employees. (In fact, if you want to know why we have a 54-hour time frame, it is because we won't begin a Startup Weekend until people are finished with work on Friday evenings.) They may be high up or lower down on the corporate ladder. They may be lawyers or designers or marketers. They may be you! But most of them think of themselves as people who have a job and a boss, and their goal, at least in the short term, is to get paid more to do that job, or to move up a step into a job that pays better.

But there's a lot more to our lives than that. So take a minute, and instead of merely thinking about what you can get paid well to do, think about what *you'd like to do* and then think about what *you can do well*.

> Imagine that you were suddenly able to get paid to do absolutely anything. What would you do? What is one small step you can perform now that will get you closer to making this dream job a reality?

This isn't a fairy tale; we're not suggesting that the life you envision can become yours magically. But breaking out of the *employee box* can be both liberating and can help you make decisions about your career that may ultimately make you happier. Becoming an entrepreneur is about determining what you'd like to do, what you can do well, and then figuring out how to get someone to pay you to do it (in that order). It requires planning, creativity, and some risk.

The entrepreneurial path is actually something like a ladder. Each rung can be harder to reach than the one before it. Of course, everyone will have their own adventures along the way, but we want to help people avoid getting stuck between the rungs. We want people to use the ladder we describe next to figure out where they are and where they're going.

The Entrepreneurship Leap

So, the first step to becoming an entrepreneur—taking the **entrepreneurship leap**—is soul-searching. But it also requires some outside research. Find out as much as you can about the world of startups. You can begin by picking up a

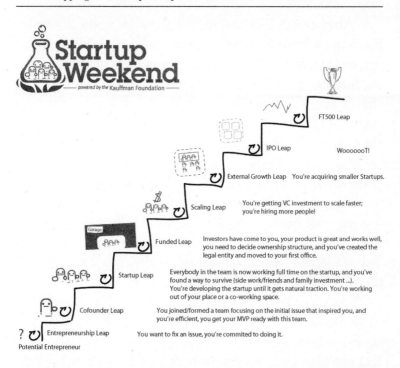

book (oh, right; you already did). There are, however, also a large number of events and projects to help you find out more about entrepreneurship. Check out Global Entrepreneurship Week, for instance. It's a Kauffman Foundation initiative, with almost half a million people in 2010 participating in over 3,200 activities to promote entrepreneurship. High schools, colleges, government agencies, and companies all support these activities, which include virtual and face-to-face events, large-scale competitions, and small networking gatherings. And that's just in the United States. There are events in more than 100 countries with 35,000 organizations around the world that are part of Global Entrepreneurship Week. The purpose of these events is not just to start new companies, though many do come out of them; the purpose is to ensure that people have ample opportunity to explore their potential as self-starters.

Other events like this include Ignite, in which partici-pants get five minutes to share an idea with a local crowd. Igniters can meet other entrepreneurs, hear about interest-ing initiatives in their hometown, and feel the kind of vibe that a room full of entrepreneurial types can offer. Or there's TED, which tries to foster the spread of new ideas through conferences and lectures around the world. There are also business-plan competitions that one can enter to get a sense of the entrepreneurial landscape. And if you want to get a feel for what these events are like without leaving your house, a number of the Global Entrepreneur-ship Week offerings and Ignite and TED events have You-Tube videos devoted to them. But really, you should get off the couch and check them out in real life. It's worth it.

You know you're an entrepreneur when you seriously think about quitting your job, when money is not your main motivation anymore, when you are driven by passion and nothing will stop you from launching something that will change the world!

The Cofounder Leap

We often get the question: Should I come to Startup Weekend if I don't have an idea to pitch? The answer is a resounding *YES!* Only one-third of Startup Weekend par-ticipants pitch an idea. While the average guy on the street may think that an entrepreneur without an idea is like a cyclist without a bike, we at Startup Weekend know the truth, which we've repeated again and again: Ideas are im-portant, but the team is essential.

The news is full of stories of the lone entrepreneur who clings tightly to his dream and works tirelessly, for years and against all odds, to prove all the naysayers wrong. We hear the Mark Zuckerbergs praised as tenacious geniuses (and they are); but that's only half of the story. Even visionaries need a team of doers to bring their paradigm-shifting, brand-new idea to life. From mentors to investors to lawyers to employees to fellow cofounders, there's a whole stream of people involved in even the most humble startup. And at Startup Weekend, we believe that the teammates who believe in each other and in a shared vision of the future have the best chance for entrepreneurial success. The underlying concept matters, of course—but only when it stands on the shoulders of a truly stellar group of people who are able to execute!

Since the team is of paramount importance—and will be even more so in the future, when access to technology, information, and resources becomes even more widely available—Startup Weekend is committed to recruiting as many of the best people to our events as we can. Currently, over half of all Startup Weekend attendees pitch an idea at our events; we'd like to increase that number in the future. While only a certain percentage of ideas are selected for team formation, we believe that as more ideas are pitched, the more innovative and committed to the entrepreneurial process attendees become. Certainly, each team can only work on one idea over the weekend. However, if each person on the team has offered an idea, then what does this say about the creative potential of each team member, whether developer, designer, or product manager?

In the future, Startup Weekend would like to do even more to support high-potential teams, regardless of their ideas, as they work to bring their startup to the next level. From our network of mentors, to our partnerships with incubators and accelerators, to our participation in momentous programs like Startup America, Startup Weekend will connect alumni to the resources they most need to move forward.

Ultimately, the best way to find out whether you have what it takes to be an entrepreneur is to meet other entrepreneurs and talk to them about what they do and what you can do. We now realize that this is something of a breakthrough, in and of itself.

{ Painters talk with other painters; athletes talk with other athletes; teachers talk with other teachers. Why shouldn't entrepreneurs talk with other entrepreneurs? }

Just a few decades ago, entrepreneurs were often based in their basements and garages, and they were usually alone. When the personal computer became a part of everyday life, coders started to meet up, but oftentimes (and we're only exaggerating slightly), it was merely to play video games and have fun programming them. The culture was still overwhelmingly male and comprised mostly of computer-based interactions. And even though folks had computers, there was no social networking; so entrepreneurs were mostly restricted to working with people in their immediate vicinity (like the guy in the garage next door). It's not that they couldn't communicate with others; it's simply that the distance made things more arduous and expensive. (Remember when we paid extra for long-distance phone calls?) Our networks used to depend more on our locality. For instance, even if we graduated from a business school on the other side of the country, it was still hard (except in a few cities) to find a critical mass of alumni with whom to work on a project.

What Startup Weekend has done is to gather people from different sorts of backgrounds—developers, businesspeople, artists, designers, lawyers, and so on—and encouraged them to talk about their common interest in entrepreneurship. It's almost as though we knocked on a lot of garage doors and got people to come out and be social.

And that is the next step in the evolution of an entrepreneur—the **cofounder leap**. This is the stage at which people have already learned more about startups and have decided it's time for them to meet the right people to get their ideas off the ground, or to get involved with someone else's idea.

This is where Startup Weekend comes in. This is when you start dating—when you find out who you like and who likes you in return. When you are new to this world of entrepreneurship, it is important not just to meet people, but also to meet the *right* people. You need to find people who have a real passion for entrepreneurship, who complement both your skill set and your personality, and who are at a point in their careers and their personal lives where they can give some time (even if it's not all their time) to launching a startup.

In addition to Startup Weekend, there are events like Coffee 2.0 meetups, Startup Drinks, Founder Dating, Women 2.0, and hundreds of local initiatives designed to help entrepreneurs get in contact with able, willing, and like-minded people.

The most important thing to keep in mind in all of these initiatives is that you have to *talk* to people, and share your ideas. There used to be a longstanding tradition among entrepreneurs that they must keep their ideas secret. People would practically walk around with nondisclosure agreements in their pockets. This is not an effective way of finding cofounders or colleagues—or even learning if your idea is worth anything. If you clam up, then the person you are talking to will clam up, too. Therefore, we encourage trust in Startup Weekend participants. Your idea won't be worth anything if you keep it to yourself, and going to Startup Weekend to chat about the weather is a total waste of everyone's time.

Meeting other people and forming a team is a great way to keep yourself motivated—to see that you don't keep making excuses for yourself. People tell us they would be launching a business if it weren't for their job, their family, their age, their place of residence, or whatever. It's natural. But we have met people in all the same circumstances who decided they'd stalled long enough and finally made a go of it—you can too.

> Cofounders who believe in another person's idea are just as important as cofounders who have an idea and are looking for another person to believe in.
>
> ■ Are you having trouble getting started with your idea?
> ■ Is your action plan appropriate given your skills, resources, and constraints?

The Startup Leap

The third step, the **startup leap,** is for people who have assembled a team and have the outlines of an idea for a business. People at this step are also good candidates to attend Startup Weekend. We have a couple of teams that are already formed but are looking for more help at many of our events. They may even have built something at a previous Startup Weekend, but need to develop their project further. These people can use the weekend as a time to advance their projects, move the idea to the next level, conduct more customer research, or find more developers or businesspeople. As long as they are looking for true team members, and not free labor, teams at the startup leap can find many essential components at Startup Weekend. It's not just the cofounder who is important to a successful startup. Charlie O'Donnell, one of Startup Weekend's advisers and a principal at First Round Capital in New York, says that getting "the first five employees right is vital." According to O'Donnell, "Figuring out the right team and getting the right people is super important." In fact, he thinks that one of the most important things a venture capitalist can do is to help a team make the right hires. A lot of people get stuck when they realize they're missing a particular skill set. O'Donnell says he can look at a mobile application, for instance, and tell teams what person they're missing. Maybe it's the sales team or the product development, or the user experience person. No matter what, he says, the plan would have been better if the entire team had been there from the beginning.

> - Do you know what skills and strengths you bring to the team?
> - Can you identify your team members' skills and strengths?
> - Can they identify yours?

People who have formed well-rounded teams at Startup Weekend seem very inclined to continue the process. Indeed, the majority of Startup Weekend participants plan to continue to work on their team's idea after the weekend, with 36 percent reporting that all of the members will continue working on the project and 41 percent reporting that some subgroup of the team will do so.

It's not only that surrounding yourself with the most competent team is vital to your success at the beginning; it is also an important contributor to how well your startup will do in the long run. You may think you enjoy being alone, but being alone means that your startup will rise and fall depending on your outlook, and no one else's.

Some days, you'll feel great. You'll be thinking, "Oh my God! I'm going to develop all these things and create the perfect product. Being an entrepreneur is awesome." Once you hit a few bumps in the road, though, you might start to feel bad. You may begin wondering, "What have I done? I'm never going to make it. These ideas are terrible."

Your mood on a particular day may seem like a trivial concern now, but believe us: *It's not*. More people on a team can create an emotional equilibrium. Not every member is going to feel good or bad at the same time. Being an entrepreneur can be tough. There are times when nobody believes in you. You have zero money. You have this vision of something you want to accomplish, but you may feel like you're not making enough progress. After six months, after a year, you don't want to be alone because you don't want to give up.

There are other parts of the startup ecosystem that can help you find the people you need for your team and the kind of support you need for your vision. Bar Camps, for instance, are user-generated conferences to discuss not only new technological innovations but also ideas about politics, health care, transportation, and a variety of other subjects. Fail Conferences offer the opportunity to hear from experienced entrepreneurs and other leaders about some of the mistakes they've made along their way to success— mistakes they're hoping to help others avoid. Both of these are great opportunities to learn more about the entrepreneurial environment, and to meet people who you might want to work with in the future.

We're living in a wonderful, but also challenging, time for entrepreneurs. The world is flatter. With greater and cheaper access to technology, most people with a dream and a computer with Internet access can reach potential consumers across the globe and begin selling their product or service with a simple website. Creating a company is no longer just the undertaking of Ivy League graduates or trust-fund babies. On the other hand, it's even harder to get your message heard and differentiate yourself from the competition with so many more people sharing their creative output. Entrepreneurs are no longer just contending with the boutique down the street; they're up against every boutique that has a web presence—even stores in countries of which they may never have heard. Experiences like Startup Weekend help participants learn fast and outsmart the competition by allowing early-stage entrepreneurs to brush up against dozens—even hundreds—of potential customers, future team members, and mentors.

You know you achieved the startup leap once people come to you asking about your awesome product. This is a good sign to start focusing on the **funded leap**. If you don't have natural traction, it's a pretty good sign that your startup needs work. Go back to customer development—customers don't lie!

The Funded Leap

Show me the money? Well, not quite yet! We realize that a lot of people will want to see the money earlier in the process of becoming an entrepreneur. They'll expect to receive some kind of funding as soon as possible. You may be wondering: Shouldn't this be step one or two? The answer is: *absolutely not*. Part of the new entrepreneurship model is that you don't need money to start. You need time, and you need people. But you don't need money.

The reason for this is that most of the startups to which we're referring are web or mobile applications that don't require any initial overhead. As one veteran entrepreneur told us:

> One great thing about Startup Weekend is that you could potentially be making money starting on day one, because attending doesn't cost much and the overhead costs for most of these tech startups are next to nothing.

While most people are not necessarily profitable from the very beginning, the point is that there is no reason to spend your money—or anyone else's, for that matter—until you have more information. Get the knowledge; *then* get the funds.

As we discussed earlier, you don't even need to actually *create* the product. You just need to give people a good enough idea of what the product is so that you can see whether they will actually buy it. You need to spend time, both during the weekend and afterward, talking to potential customers and testing out different versions of the idea. Don't just throw a bunch of stuff at the wall and see what sticks; throw individual pieces at the wall. If something doesn't stick, examine it, cook it a little more and then throw it again.

This will take place very quickly—and it *should*. Starting a business will happen faster than you think, maybe even over the course of a weekend. Two in five Startup

Weekend participants believe that their team's idea could be ready for launch (defined as a first sale or transaction or the sale of the idea to a third party) in one to three months, while 28 percent believe that their idea could be ready in less than a month, and 19 percent believe that their team will need four to six months to ready their idea.

This is great news, not only in the sense that you want to get to the funded leap quickly but also because you won't waste time. Your time is worth something, and you shouldn't spend it working on an idea that's not going anywhere. If you use the techniques we've discussed in earlier chapters, we think you'll find that you'll get to success—or to failure—much more quickly. And if you get to failure, you can move on to the next idea and find success.

The Scaling Leap

So, let's say you've assembled your team and done your research. Perhaps you've won Startup Weekend or were voted the "idea most likely to make a million dollars." Let's say you have the validation of the 150 people with whom you spent the weekend. What's the next step?

There are several programs out there that do *mentoring incubation*; that is, they will help to support entrepreneurs both financially and educationally for a few weeks or months to see if their ideas take off. These programs are not easy to get into; however, once you're in, you have the freedom and the mentor expertise at your disposal to really pursue your project full-time and wholeheartedly. Y-Combinator, Tech Stars, and Startup Labs are all great entry points into the world of Startup Funding.

This is the stage at which somebody—an outsider— really starts to believe in your dream. That's when you can move closer to jumping off the entrepreneurial cliff.

This brings us to the next step in the entrepreneurial ladder—the **scaling leap**. Venture capitalists are constantly considering the groups and individuals that come out of the programs we just mentioned. While the people who complete those programs don't automatically get seed funding, many of them do. Meeting the right mentors in those programs can be a ticket to finding financial support.

We do want to pause here to say that not every startup needs venture capital. In fact, very few Fortune 500 companies actually take venture capital money. Many of them experience natural growth that is sustainable over time *without* money coming in from investors. They get regular income from customers instead, and then put that back into the business. But there are certain kinds of companies that can only scale up if they get some infusion of capital from outside. Maybe your team needs to hire more staff or purchase a better server, or perhaps you've outgrown the garage space your family allotted you.

External Growth Leap

Once you have scaled up, your success will be fairly obvious both to you and to your competitors. This indicates that it's time for the next step—the **external growth leap**. This is when you begin to think about acquiring some of the competition, or having them acquire you. For instance, a number of businesses have launched using the Groupon model of group-buying specials and have subsequently been bought out by Groupon. Others will still try to compete with Groupon on a smaller scale, perhaps occupying a niche market. Different entrepreneurs have different feelings about being acquired—that is, exiting the market at this point. Some will see it as success; they walk away with some hefty sum of money. But others will be disappointed that they didn't take their company further. Entrepreneurs can be sentimental, too, and become very attached to both their ideas and their team.

The next steps for those who do go on are the **IPO leap** and the **Fortune 500 leap**. Though these are not common occurrences, they do happen—and they are an important part of the startup ecosystem. Entrepreneurs who have made it this far can turn around and become mentors to those coming up the ladder. They can provide seed capital to teams that are just starting out, and they also provide a representation to the outside world of what a driven entrepreneur can accomplish. We want to create an ecosystem that can support more billion-dollar companies being created.

Leaping More Often

This model is something we have been working on at Startup Weekend for a while now. We believe it is a good place to start. It gives all of us in the entrepreneurial community a common understanding by which to judge how well we are doing at encouraging the formation of startups. We can see, for instance, whether people are getting stuck on a particular step and determine whether we can add resources to help them.

In our experience, a lot of people get stuck between the entrepreneurship leap and the funded leap, because they tend to skip over the cofounder leap. They are keeping their ideas to themselves. They are not sure how to form a team or where to find the right people. We see this as an important niche for Startup Weekend. But we'd also like to get more groups that have already formed to take part in Startup Weekend—recruiting more of the new talent and listening to fresh perspectives, as well as helping them progress with projects on which they are already working.

Startup Weekend's greatest impact can be felt on the community level. As much as we like to think about entrepreneurship as a global phenomenon (and it is) and as much as we like to think about entrepreneurs from all over the world being in contact with each other (and they are), we have found that some of the most interesting developments in entrepreneurship are taking place at the local level. With all of the technology available that allows us to communicate with people on the other side of the world, we have lost sight of how important face-to-face communication can be. Indeed, it is vital to the exchange of ideas, the formation of teams, and the growth of startups.

> Have you felt the impact of affecting a larger community? How does affecting an entire community differ from affecting only one or two people?

Right now, entrepreneurs and people interested in entrepreneurship are frequently alone—or feel they are alone. Startup communities and their associated programs and initiatives are often fragmented, broken, or nonexistent, which makes it difficult for aspiring entrepreneurs to find the resources and support they need, when they need it.

On a higher level, institutions and some older programs have extended the myths of entrepreneurship. Therefore, they ultimately do not contribute to the creation of successful ventures or a culture supportive of true entrepreneurship. They continue to suggest that a good idea is the most important part of a business. They encourage budding entrepreneurs to keep their ideas close to the vest, and they worry about who has the rights to some piece of intellectual property—and all this before a company is even launched.

In order to combat this kind of thinking, Startup Weekend is trying to figure out not only how to bring more events to more people in more places, but also how to have a more permanent presence in those communities. How can we build an entrepreneurial culture over time, and not just over a weekend?

For one thing, we'd like to coordinate with other members of the entrepreneurial ecosystem. We want to institute events that prepare entrepreneurs for Startup Weekend and help to support them afterward. We will be having reunion events for people who have participated in the past.

We are also trying to incorporate even more networking during the course of the weekend. Perhaps merely working with the people on your team doesn't provide enough exposure to the talents of the other Startup Weekend attendees. We have been trying a variety of games and contests that will encourage people to do more mingling at future events.

We also want everyone who has participated in a weekend to be able to tap into the entire entrepreneurial network. So we are going to be trying some cross-pollination—sending folks from San Francisco to Chile or from Cairo to New York or Brazil to Tunisia—to allow participants to learn more about the global startup experience. Perhaps this will give them ideas for how to maneuver around some of the onerous regulations that small organizations face, or help them figure out how to expand their business ideas on an international level. What with the world being so flat and all. . . . Well, you get the picture.

The Future of Startup Weekend

Coming together and experiencing a Startup Weekend gets people asking themselves and others: *What's next?* In the past, we haven't been able to supply any kind of support after Startup Weekends, but time and again we watch people come out Monday morning and say, "What's next?" The more people who ask that question, the better—because that question creates the need for more programs and initiatives to help answer it. This, in turn, helps fuel the entrepreneurial revolution from the bottom up.

There is a lot of talk these days about how we encourage entrepreneurship from the top down, whether you work for the government, you're a venture capitalist, a politician, a civil servant, or you're in academia. People constantly ask themselves how they can put this entrepreneurship stuff on top of existing programs and reap the benefits. But none of these plans seem to work. The truth is that it has to be seeded from the grassroots level to succeed.

At Startup Weekend, we are trying to bring people from different parts of the ecosystem together. Over the past few years, high-level people in government and business have been talking at events like the Davos Forum. But those kinds of events weren't attracting the senior CEOs or CTOs from the successful companies in a particular town. And those senior business people weren't meeting the hungry entrepreneurs on the ground who are still at the beginning stages of their careers.

We're finding that the Startup Weekend experience is just as educational for the people on the top rungs of the ecosystem. The more entrepreneurs who get the chance to talk with investors, the more programs investors will create to support those entrepreneurs, and the more entrepreneurs who are then going to be attracted into the programs. We are hoping for, and expecting, this kind of a snowball effect.

The Startup Foundation

In the future, we hope to expand Startup Weekend's influence by forming something called the Startup Foundation. We aim to make this initiative the world's most powerful way to invest in the development of an entrepreneurial community and ecosystem. By focusing on particular cities and towns, we hope to help entrepreneurs meet each other and work together more frequently. This will foster creativity, innovation, and new business creation on a grassroots level. By empowering community leaders across a global network, we can maximize impact, learn from our efforts, and unify on a large scale.

With the support of the Kauffman Foundation, we are planning to appoint Startup Cofounders in eight cities around the world. These leaders will coordinate the efforts of various startup events and try to bring more of these kinds of events to their particular areas. The Startup Cofounders will try to connect disparate groups, including university student organizations, corporations, coworking spaces, chambers of commerce, investors, and so on.

Educating people about what it takes to become an entrepreneur, as well as the great things that entrepreneurship can do for a community, is going to be vital for the Startup Foundation. We want to create more startup evangelists who will bring their friends and colleagues to the network. One of the reasons Startup Weekend has been so successful is that we get people from an extensive variety of backgrounds to come to our events. But we want to cast our net even more widely. We want to promote the kind of curriculum we talked about in Chapter 4—a curriculum of best practices for entrepreneurs. In partnership with people like Steve Blank and Carl Schramm, we are working on ways to spread these ideas through social media, mentoring programs, and even individual blogs as a platform for sharing successes. We have to get the message out there in as many ways as possible.

Another important aspect of this work is our attempt to gain more information about the way startups are formed. Although we've conducted extensive research while tracking Startup Weekend participants' progress over time, there is still a lot we have to learn. One of the key roles that the Startup Foundation sees itself fulfilling is to build a database of information about how startups are formed and how individual entrepreneurs evolve. We would also like to conduct more in-depth analysis of the impact of entrepreneurial activity on job creation.

We will be rolling out the Startup Foundation in eight cities in 2012, and then continue expanding in 2013. This will be a test for us. Ideally, we'd like to see a Startup Cofounder coordinating these efforts in every major city in the United States and in other places around the world. We want to determine whether it's possible to improve the outcomes for individual entrepreneurs by strengthening the overall entrepreneurial community, and to see if there are ways in which we can help people on their startup journeys. So, if you hear a knock at your garage door soon, you'll know who it is!

Conclusion

Viva la Revolution

There is a startup revolution currently taking place. Many people are wondering if it's just another bubble. There is probably a bubble and it will burst. But the startup revolution is based on structural and sustainable changes in technology and business. As venture capitalist Charlie O'Donnell says, "There has never been so much content and so many resources available for entrepreneurs. If you're looking to start something there's no excuse for you to be uninformed." Rather than becoming frustrated while trying to develop ideas alone, you can actually find out about the kinds of things that venture capitalists are willing to fund. Many venture capital firms have blogs that describe particular models that are of interest to them. The whole system has become much more transparent recently.

In fact, if you went back just 15 years, you'd find most of the innovation happening in university labs. Some graduate students would be developing a new chip, and if a venture capital firm had a relationship with that lab, the firm might fund the project. Nowadays, however, there are an infinite number of places where innovation can happen. Anyone can code something over the weekend. The investors have to be out there talking to people; they can't just have good relationships with three local science labs.

There is a democratization of entrepreneurship going on today, and it starts with the technology. Having something like Google Apps, or setting up a domain and e-mail server, allows you to have a website up and running in a mere 10 or 15 minutes. Access to tools like these used to be prohibitive for most entrepreneurs just five years ago, but not anymore.

Then there are all the instruments out there that help people who launch companies gain validation. The evolution of online advertising—as well as the ability to send out Facebook ads—leverage your social networks, and gain customer feedback has been critical to this shift in the landscape as well. The cost of getting a set of eyeballs to look at your product is drastically lower nowadays. As a result, even traditional media and marketing outlets have become more accessible. Print media and television want to know what's hot out there, and so they follow the trends on social media closely.

But there are even larger forces at work here. There used to be more of a sense that if you wanted a white-collar job after high school, you should go to college. After college, you would either get a job at a company or get more schooling and become a doctor or a lawyer. It was much more of a rigid structure. However, a rise of the creative class has taken place in recent years, and the startup culture has both benefited from and contributed to this trend. There are all of these questions that people can ask themselves: We now have the luxury of being able to say, "Hey, wait a minute. What am I good at? What do I want to do? I don't have to be a doctor or a lawyer to be considered successful."

Conversations around the world are changing on this subject as we're realizing that jobs are not always created by big companies. So the dream of graduating and going to work for Google and then spending your tenure there until you can hopefully get a halfway decent management position is simply not necessary.

In part, the Great Recession has caused some of this shift in thinking. Alexis Ringwald, a Startup Weekend winner who travels the world extolling the benefits of entrepreneurship, explains it in the following way: "I think Americans have been shaken out of their complacency. They now realize that not everyone can just become an investment banker, or consultant, but that people need to create their own jobs."

Ringwald didn't come from a family of entrepreneurs; they were artists and educators. Therefore, the whole concept of starting your own business was foreign to her. "I didn't know anything about business until I was in India [and] I met the guy who would become my cofounder. He was a Silicon Valley entrepreneur and that's how we started our company, and I learned a lot through that." She says that even during her time as an undergraduate at Yale, the idea of going off on your own to start a business after graduation was considered out of the mainstream.

She tells audiences around the world to attend Startup Weekend not only because it's like "going to entrepreneurship school," but also because it builds confidence: "It kind of reminded me to be more courageous . . . and it made me realize even within two days you can start something that could change the world."

Confidence is also something that Ringwald thinks many Americans could use more of right now: "A lot of people are being laid off in the U.S. and there are high levels of unemployment; I think it takes a huge toll on your self-confidence when you lose your job. You just think you're not worth anything, your skills have no value, you can't contribute, [and] you have nothing to offer." Ringwald therefore believes that entrepreneurship can contribute in a huge way to help those people who have been laid off. They can come to something like Startup Weekend and "be reminded that their skills can contribute to some project in some small way."

Ringwald has high hopes for Startup Weekend: "It just . . . restores people's dignity, which I think is really critical as people are not finding jobs over long period[s] of time and [gradually become] more and more depressed about it." She thinks that the entrepreneurship revolution that is occurring "can have a huge effect on the national consciousness if it really penetrates some of the regions of the U.S. where so many jobs have been lost."

And there is real potential outside of the United States. Startup Weekend is not just operating in Western Europe; we are going to countries from Nigeria to Tunisia to Russia to Chile to Lebanon. Creating jobs in these less-wealthy, less-developed countries will hopefully spur their economies and perhaps even create greater political stability. As you may have heard, the world's never been so flat. It doesn't really matter who you are or where you are. We can all benefit from being able to access other people—other potential teammates—around the world.

As Ringwald says, "I think Startup Weekend could be the new form of diplomacy. Rather than sending troops, we should be nurturing entrepreneurs in other countries because when people are starting businesses and starting livelihoods they have less incentive to want to fight wars and cause terror in different places." We can use American experience and know-how to foster entrepreneurs in war-pending and developing countries. She claims, "It would be great to take the model and really focus on some countries where there's a lot of devastation and try and help people create sustainable livelihoods."

So, the entrepreneurial revolution is the result of technology, as well as large-scale economic and social changes. But there are other factors at play, too—like the development of a pool of risk capital. Investors are now willing to make bets on startups in a way they have never been before.

And then there is also a new understanding of what it takes to make a startup succeed. The work done by people like Steve Blank has ensured that entrepreneurs don't need to just rely on luck in order to be successful. There is a process now and a real understanding of how entrepreneurs can mitigate their risk and grow at the right pace into something great. It is really important to get into the flow of using best practices, to understand how to test things out, and to learn from people who have done this before.

The Entrepreneur Culture

The whole environment for entrepreneurs is changing. The very word *entrepreneur* has become more commonly used by people on the street. While there is still much to be done in terms of bringing other professions into this— in particular, academics and law—a good amount of progress has been made. Big business has even begun to notice where innovation is coming from. Some large corporations are aiming to create a kind of startup environment in their own offices, using some of the tools of project management we talked about in Chapter 5.

However, they have also begun to realize that since startups are so effective at doing this kind of innovation, they might not have to do as much themselves. Nick Seguin at the Kauffman Foundation says he has found many large businesses moving away from large R&D investments and instead trying to acquire the technology created by the startups or even trying to acquire the startups themselves. Yet, these developments also mean that larger companies now have a stake in the startups' success, and have therefore started to pay more attention to this startup ecosystem.

So has the media. There have been articles in every major newspaper and magazine, on every major TV and radio station about the importance of startups. They are often feel-good local stories about how one person's idea was able to change the community for the better. But are those kinds of stories enough to change the culture?

As much as we talk about ingenuity and innovation being part of the United States' DNA, there's still that funny look that some people get when you're introducing your husband or your wife around the circle—in which everybody else is an investment banker or in marketing—and you say something like, "Yeah, he's working on his own thing right now." It's simply not part of the cultural norm. There are always psychological and social aspects of being an entrepreneur. If we could get a critical mass of people engaged in entrepreneurship, or at least *know* someone who is an entrepreneur, then the barrier to entry might seem a little lower.

Your Next Iteration

Startup Weekend serves different functions for different people. Startup Weekend is helping entrepreneurs reach the next step in their respective journeys, wherever they currently are on the startup ladder. For those who know what they're doing, the weekend offers a condensed chronological period in which to get things done. They know they can access people, focus solely on things related to their entrepreneurial vision over that weekend, and actually launch something. Startup Weekend is the obvious next step in their development as entrepreneurs.

For others, Startup Weekend is a community builder. It's simply a way to meet people, and even if you walk away with no fully formed companies after the weekend, at least

70 people who didn't know each other before now do. And who knows what could come out of that at some point down the line? Maybe a couple of years from now when one person from that weekend gets involved in a new company, he or she will call the team and ask if anyone is interested in a new opportunity.

For others, and this is specifically true when we're running in less entrepreneurial communities or cities, especially in places like Eastern Europe, for instance, Startup Weekend is a proof point that you can work on something and not work on it after the weekend. The culture of which you are a part hasn't really accepted the legitimacy of entrepreneurship, but eventually it might, and you could be one of the early adapters. In the meantime, your experience has helped you learn something about your skills and exposed you to a global network of entrepreneurs. Maybe you'll decide that it's time to explore entrepreneurship somewhere else, or that you're going to be the person who starts to change the culture surrounding you.

No matter into which of these categories you might fall, Startup Weekend will help you try out new versions of yourself. It doesn't just let you change your business model or your product over the course of 48 hours; it allows you to alter how you see yourself. And trying out entrepreneurship can be a life-changing experience.

Seguin recalls meeting four derivatives traders at the last Startup Weekend in New York. "That's a big tough job; you're making a lot of money, and you're not really sleeping that much. But for some reason, these four came out this weekend and stayed up until 3 [AM] and were back at 9 [AM] each day." The reason is clear, actually: Startup Weekend is a chance to try something new. You don't get a lot of those opportunities in life because of what you're doing during the day or what your commitments are to family and so forth. Your boss might even be upset if he found out you had 54 hours free over the weekend. (We won't tell!)

Individuals trying out new versions of themselves eventually form new kinds of communities. If you spend a little time in the world of entrepreneurship, you'll start to hear people say of each other, "Oh, I met so-and-so at Startup Weekend."

Over time, Startup Weekend will continue to create loose ties among people who have some interest in entrepreneurship, and it will create strong ties as well. Startup Weekend has formed a kind of nexus of people in communities who are really committed to making the startup ecosystem work.

We all have a tendency to look at the big players in an economy—government, big business, super-wealthy philanthropists—and assume that they will make or break the eventual success of our community and our world. But now there is a willing and able global network of people who are committed to the startup model. These entrepreneurs—all entrepreneurs—are the most powerful force for good in the world.

Further Readings

NOTE: THE FOLLOWING materials are those that we have found particularly useful during our entrepreneurial journey and are not intended to be a comprehensive list.

Books

- J. Bacon, *The Art of Community: Building the New Age of Participation (Theory in Practice)* (Sebastopol, CA: O'Reilly Media, Inc., 2009).
- S. Belsky, *Making Ideas Happen: Overcoming the Obstacles Between Vision and Reality* (New York: Penguin Group, 2010).
- A. Bhide, *The Origin and Evolution of New Businesses* (New York: Oxford University Press, 2003).
- S. Blank, *The Four Steps to the Epiphany: Successful Strategies for Products that Win* (San Mateo, CA: CafePress.com, 2005).
- J. Fried, *Getting Real: The Smarter, Faster, Easier Way to Build a Successful Web Application* (Chicago: 37signals, LLC., 2009).
- J. Fried, *Rework* (Chicago: 37signals, LLC., 2010).
- S. Godin, *Linchpin: Are You Indispensable?* (New York: Penguin Group, 2010).
- T. Hsieh, *Delivering Happiness: A Path to Profits, Passion, and Purpose* (New York: Hachette Book Group, 2010).
- G. Kawasaki, *Art of the Start: The Time-Tested, Battle-Hardened Guide for Anyone Starting Anything* (New York: Penguin Group, 2004).
- J. Livingston, *Founders at Work: Stories of Startups' Early Days* (New York: Springer-Verlag, 2007).

- J. Medina, *Brain Rules: 12 Principles for Surviving and Thriving at Work, Home, and School* (Seattle: Pear Press, 2008).
- J. Rasmusson, *The Agile Samurai: How Agile Masters Deliver Great Software* (Raleigh, NC: Pragmatic Programmers, LLC., 2010).

Blogs and Other Media

- "10 Inspiring TED Talks for Startups"
  http://www.readwriteweb.com/start/2010/07/ten-inspiring-ted-talks-for-st.php
- Jeff Bussgang, "Seeing Both Sides"
  http://bostonvcblog.typepad.com/vc/2009/11/what-makes-bostons-startup-scene-special.html
- Tom Chapman, "Building an Entrepreneurial Ecosystem: Lessons from Omaha"
  http://www.scribd.com/doc/60113134/Building-an-Entrepreneurial-Ecosystem-Lessons-from-Omaha
- Brad Feld, "Feld Thoughts"
  http://www.feld.com/wp/
- William Fisher, "View from the Fishbowl: Noodling" (Silicon Prairie News)
  http://www.siliconprairienews.com/2011/06/view-from-the-fishbowl-noodling
- Daniel Isenberg, "How to Start an Entrepreneurial Ecosystem" (HBR blog network)
  http://hbr.org/product/how-to-start-an-entrepreneurial-revolution/an/R1006A-HCB-ENG
- Eric Koester, "Zaarly on Capitol Hill: Why the Startup Ecosystem Matters"
  http://www.xconomy.com/seattle/2011/05/13/zaarly-on-capitol-hill-why-the-startup-ecosystem-matters/

- Sarah Lacy, "Predictably Rabid: The Life and Times of Sarah Lacy"
  http://www.sarahlacy.com/sarahlacy/2008/07/the-post-gets-m.html
- 37signals, "The Slicehost Story"
  http://37signals.com/svn/posts/2974-the-slicehost-story

Index